# Your Personal Tool Kit for Life

FACING A MAJOR LIFE RENOVATION AND
CONSTRUCTING THE BEST LIFE POSSIBLE

# Your Personal Tool Kit for Life

## Facing a Major Life Renovation and Constructing the Best Life Possible

LARA WIBETO

MILL CITY PUBLISHING
MINNEAPOLIS, MN

Copyright © 2010 by Lara Wibeto.

Mill City Press, Inc.
212 3rd Avenue North, Suite 290
Minneapolis, MN 55401
612.455.2294
www.millcitypublishing.com

All rights reserved. No part of this publication may be reproduced, stored in a retrieval system, or transmitted, in any form or by any means, electronic, mechanical, photocopying, recording, or otherwise, without the prior written permission of the author.

ISBN - 978-1-936107-51-3
ISBN - 1-936107-51-1
LCCN - 2010920384

Cover Design by Wes Moore
Typeset by James Arneson

*Printed in the United States of America*

I dedicate this book to my beloved friend Russell. I have done what you always pushed me to do: to relate my life story and how I repaired myself when I was broken, in order to help others. You inspired me to stay strong when my body and spirit were damaged. I can still hear you on the telephone telling me to "Go for it." Thank you for always believing in me. Your uplifting wisdom and enthusiasm were an inspiration to so many men and women including me. It was an honor and a blessing to have had your optimism in my life when you were in this world.

# CONTENTS

*Introduction*     1

1. There are weak links in my chain of friends and family. It's time to find stronger ones     3

2. Put your hard hat on. There's heavy fallout ahead.     6

3. I know I left my Self-Esteem somewhere. Where's that stud finder?     8

4. Emergency Self-Esteem Box for Personal Tool Kit: Creating a self-esteem boosting system that works.     11

5. Your Personal Crisis List for Major Disrepair     14

6. Get out the hammer and chisel. You have serious corrosion and it shows!     17

7. My battery is dead. Has anyone seen my jumper cables?     23

8. Substandard thoughts create self-doubt and accidents.     25

9. Help, I think I have a screw loose! How I survived sudden illness.     28

10. Where is that duct tape? The Scotch tape holding my life together isn't working.     49

11. My last oil change was a long time ago and my engine is running dirty.     69

12. Changing gear with a different career     110

13. Somebody notices that I have the best tools for success in life and love.     118

14. How do you reset this panic button on my alarm system?     178

15. Any product that claims it lasts forever better have a lifetime warranty.     180

16. I have the best tools for the job. Don't tell me that I can't do it!     189

17. No female part is exactly alike. Male parts are no more important than female ones.     196

18. My engine is revved up. I'm ready to run.     209

19. There has to be something in my tool kit that will prevent clogs in my dream machine.     216

20. Effectively maintaining your superstructure by using Your Personal Tool Kit for Life.     218

# INTRODUCTION

"You always had the power to go back to Kansas. Close your eyes, click your heels together three times and think to yourself, 'There's no place like home.'" - Glinda, Good Witch of the North, *The Wizard of Oz*, MGM, 1939.

Just like Dorothy, you already have the tools necessary to get to that place where you want to, and need to, be. First, you have to pinpoint what the problem is, that thing that has to be repaired in your life. Then you will have to acquire the tools necessary to do the repair work. I hope you will create your personal tool kit for life, making sure to use the correct tools for the job.

Let's get to work.

What's in the way of reaching your dreams or goals? Is it a person, a personal problem, a health issue, a group of peers, a family member, or a group of family members? Is the obstacle financial, geographical, or simply that you cannot see yourself getting to your chosen destination in life? Are you too worried about getting somebody else to their destination without considering what is most important to you? Stop right there and listen to what your gut is telling you. That's right. You need to focus on yourself. Forget about what others have told you that you could or could not do. You are going to do whatever it is that you must do in order to reach your personal goals.

Nothing and no one can stand in your way. If somebody tries to stand in your way, find a way to keep on walking past them without blinking an eye, leaving them in complete awe of your rediscovered self-confidence. You were not created to spin your wheels or wander aimlessly in life, not for anyone or anything. Stop idling, pull yourself up by the boot straps (or ankle straps for the fashionistas out there) and take a close look at your life. What are you doing to make YOU happy? What are YOU doing that makes you miserable? Albert Einstein once said that insanity is "doing the same thing over and over and expecting different results." Stop repeating the same ineffective processes in your daily life that are making you feel run down or broken. Start being good to yourself for once. If you are a caregiver type, you are always doing for others, lost in their needs and ignoring your own. You cannot be strong for anyone until you first address your needs and are operating within your strongest self possible.

## Chapter One

There are weak links in my chain of friends and family. It's time to find stronger ones.

Please stay away from people who insult you, people who interfere with what you are doing to make yourself happy, and anyone who generally makes you feel badly about yourself. Limit contact with these individuals whenever possible. You know who they are. They are the doubters, naysayers, verbal abusers, humiliators, and human wrecking balls in your life. It is wise to avoid any one of these taser-tongued destroyers who make you feel small, ineffective, or inadequate. Who needs those insensitive advohaters anyway? You are way too strong to put up with that nonsense. You will become stronger as soon as you decide to live life for yourself and not every other person with you as the exception.

You can never be too busy to live for yourself. That's right. You can handle your relationship, family, and career responsibilities without completely forgetting who you are and what makes you happy. What do you love to do the most? This is probably what you should pursue for a career. Whatever that talent is, that thing that you do best, you must develop it. Learn how to optimize this skill set while striving to always do your personal best. This is how I live day to day while maintaining peace of mind. I remain true to myself without going over the weight limit of this world's problems by dealing with each issue separately and only as needed.

Some of the people in your life will get in your way if you let them. Do not go there. Once you take those few liberating steps forward, keep moving forward. People who operate against your personal goals will slowly kill your spirit if you start to backslide. I have seen this happen to friends and family members along the way. This ugly cycle of self-destruction is one of the most heartbreaking to witness. You know the action that you must first take to start living for you. Forget the old "I don't have any money" or "I have no spare time" excuses. These excuses are meaningless in the pursuit of what you really want in life. You have the tools within your reach. You must find them and learn to use them properly to make your life work for you. It is time to make it happen.

If somebody is keeping you from doing whatever it is that you are great at and enjoy doing, you must get away from this person. Tell this person that he or she must accept the real you, not some vision that she or he has of you. He or she must share the vision that you have of your life and your expectations for the future. Do you see it now? Are you ready to conjure up the very essence of your being? Are you prepared to accept the fallout of your decision to move forward with your dreams, no matter what? I am happy for you. I know you can do it. The hardest part is to see where you are in pursuit of your dreams. Are you ready to let go of the past, remembering its lessons learned? Are you prepared to go all the way back to yourself? Great! Let's roll. I am positive that this new and improved vessel that you createthis journey will transport you to a better place in life than the one that you are currently in. Let's examine your closest relationships. Who makes you feel great no matter how near or far from this person you are? These men and women are your true friends. Work to maintain these relationships to the men and women who think you are wonderful no matter what your situation in life may be. True friendships are the relationships worth maintaining. Hopefully these relationships last for a very, very long time throughout your life. Amazingly, you will meet more and more of these similarly-minded kindred spirits along the way, especially when you are following your dreams. I believe that we are meant to meet these people, these friends that are always there for us when we need them or when life gets rough.

These are the living guardian angels that many refer to lightly. I am fortunate to have had, and to still have, these guardian angel-type friends, family members, co-workers, and supporters who read me well. These are the people in my life that know what I need without having to explain anything. You must have at least one of this type of relationship to move forward. I say this because my guardian angels in life have been with me my entire life, some I am close friends with, some are trusted colleagues, and I live ,others have moved on to another place or dimension. Some helped me through the baby steps as I had times in my life when my self-esteem was tested and I needed that extra push to keep moving forward with my dreams. These individuals provide me the support required to keep my self-esteem in excellent working condition and offer their much respected and appreciated assistance and recommendations.

It is alright to be fearful of having to depend mostly on yourself for a change. This is the only way to get to that self-chosen destination. Aren't you tired of letting others tell you where to go? It is time to let others know where you are getting off and how you are going to proceed. Those who truly care about you will support you because they know that you are headed to the place that makes you the happiest possible. You will be much happier and more put together than you thought you could be. I know these things because when you are once again in control, nobody else can control you.

## Chapter Two

Put your hard hat on.
There's heavy fallout ahead.

You have the key to the future that you have been spending all of that time and energy trying to find. Some of going on this path to your dreams is going to scare you so badly that you will want to give up. There will be days when you do not think you can take one more second of this "road less traveled," asking yourself, "Why am I making this so hard on myself?" You will begin to wonder if the doubters were correct in their assumptions of your quest for happiness. Should you stay in permanent frustrationville, never able to see the bright side of a situation? No, you cannot stay there, not for one more second. A brighter side of life truly exists. It can be a long, at times very painful, trip to personal satisfaction and self-actualization. Getting back to the real you is no walk in the park. Letting go of the broken machinery in your life that has kept you broken down is going to be the hardest thing that you have ever done. But, in the name of personal gratification, you are going to do it! OK? Let's move on. The fallout of your newfound train of thought is going to hit you when you least expect it. You will deal with this fallout in a non-destructive and timely fashion because you never get wasted time or energy back. Stop letting negativity soak it all up.

How many times have you heard yourself or somebody else say, "I can't do this. It is too difficult"? How many times has this person been you? Every time you do this to yourself, ask yourself "What is in my way? Who is in my way? How can I get back to the path that was getting me to what I wanted in the first place?" These questions are what you always need to be asking yourself in order to maintain control over your life and get you the required tools to get you where you want to be.

Let's talk about physical limitations. Do you have an illness that others told you would keep you from the things you want most? Is there an issue with your personal appearance that is holding you back emotionally? We all have physical limitations. You have to learn to overcome them, no matter how painful or annoying the reality of your illness or disability may be. Recognize what needs fixing by writing down what you are feeling or dealing with and who you think can help you. Research what is out there to help you acquire the proper tools that you need to achieve your goal and to repair problem areas in your life. Once you identify what is broken in you or your life, you can begin to locate the tools you need to repair you *and* your life.

Be realistic. Your current goal may be unattainable at this time. For example, "I want to walk, but am unable to do so." It is OK to want something which you cannot have immediately. I believe that there is still a way for you to walk, just not on the two legs you may not currently have the use of. You have your mind, your dreams, and you know what you want. Your dreams will move you, no matter what, to the place that you need to be.

*Chapter Three*

I know I left my Self-Esteem somewhere. Where's that stud finder?

"How do I keep myself motivated to succeed even though almost everyone is telling me to give up?" Ignore negative criticism. The only type of criticism that you need to listen to is the constructive kind. This type of input from others is necessary to achieve your goals or dreams. Your dreams are not like anyone else's. "How are they different you ask?" Your dreams are yours and yours alone. You may share bits and pieces of them with others along the way, but ultimately they are all about you. That is correct. Being selfish and self-serving can be the most liberating thing in the world. It may even save your life if you are as low as you can humanly stand being. It is acceptable and appropriate to use selfishness as a form of self-preservation and self-fulfillment. These are the times when if you do not do that thing that makes you happy as soon as possible, you will combust, self-destruct, go off the deep end, and completely lose control of yourself. You are strong. You must keep making progress. You were meant to be happy. I found the best wall hanging that read "Happiness happens when the door that you thought was closed, opens" and gave it to my brother for a wedding gift. Unhappiness is what happens when you stop doing all things that are pleasurable to you and bring you satisfaction.

The rewards are huge when you begin working hard to achieve that goal that you alone have set for yourself.

Who cares if you are the shortest, tallest, youngest, oldest, richest, or poorest at this instant? These qualities are all subjective and self-doubt simply isn't allowed as you acquire the tools to fill your personal tool kit. Haven't you had enough of overwhelming self-doubt? You will regain your strength once you repair your life and begin enjoying it again. Self-fulfillment is not reserved for only the rich and powerful, both of which are characteristics that are not assured to bring personal satisfaction although popular culture tells us so. Self-fulfillment is for us all to enjoy. It is the repair work in getting there that is so heart-wrenching that most people will remain un-fulfilled, half-broken, and will continue spinning their sad wheels in the same miserable place.

Whenever I meet someone who is sad and falling to pieces, I ask myself, "Why is this person losing hope for happiness?" Nobody and nothing can take your spirit and happiness away from you unless you allow them to. Stop giving others permission to crush your hopes with a sledge hammer and scatter your dreams to the wind. You have overcome too much already. Make a list of every time in your life that you felt hopeless or like you had no control. Make a list of all of the odds that you felt were against you or when you felt like there was no way out of a counterproductive situation. What or who got you through those cracks in the foundation of your life? Who or what held you together in one piece? Who was there when you needed their help to do your repair work?

Remember how you successfully overcame each obstacle and do it all over again. Leave all self-destructiveness out of the repair process. Take along with you only the tools that were effective in helping put yourself back together. Make this list of things that you've done well to help you to regain strength and get you back on your feet again. Take these coping strategies with you, in a small list, and these are tools you will use in the future if similar repair work needs to be repeated in the future.

You have officially begun creating your personal tool kit for life.

If you forget just how resilient, super-charged, and fully operational you can be, get out this list of successful coping activities from your tool kit. This preventative maintenance of positively gathering up past successes is not only productive, but essential to keeping you primed to move forward in life with your life goals and dreams.

*Chapter Four* ———————————————————

# Emergency Self-Esteem Box for Personal Tool Kit: Creating a self-esteem boosting system that works.

Have you ever had one of those days when you feel like a complete failure, that everything you touch or do amounts to a pile of sawdust? Then you need a self-esteem box. Find a preferably waterproof container such as a plastic storage bin or a large cardboard box like one you would send through the mail or with a removable lid. A storage chest will also work nicely. If you are short on space, place small items into a small container such as a shoe box with a lid. You can waterproof these containers if necessary with a roll or two of mailing tape. Remember, if all you have is a large zip loc container, than choose smaller items that will fit into the Ziploc. Be creative and try to make the container water resistant in order not to destroy moisture sensitive contents. It doesn't have to cost you a penny, but its value is immeasurable.

Delve into your personal belongings. Select only items that make you feel good about yourself. These items can be a kind note from another person, a thank-you card, an occasion card, an award, a certificate, a degree, a baby bracelet, an item of jewelry, a photo of yourself with a loved one, a photo of a loved one, a letter of appreciation, an account of a positive life-changing event, or any other item that makes you feel great about yourself. Choose small items that make you feel great about yourself and your positive qualities. Look for items that indicate the positive impact that you have had on others' lives. Make sure that the container or space is large enough if you are including items such as yearbooks, wedding albums, a photo collection, or any objects that you have collected related to life events that made you happy.

Do not keep any item that makes you feel badly about yourself or is a reminder of a time period or person from your past that you would rather not have visual reminders of. Throw this kind of thing away. If the item is deeply personal, shred it. If it is lethargic to burn it in a fireplace, destroy with power tools, or tear it to pieces, then I suggest you do that. You will feel such relief when you dispose of these horrible moments and situations in your life. You'll wonder why you didn't do this sooner.  One example of the things I got rid of after my husband and I got married were all of his old photos of his ex-wife and their former marriage. It was bad enough having to deal with her in person, never mind having to look at her image in my home. I burnt and cut up every letter and photo, and threw away anything bought by her or that she intentionally failed to take with her. I believe she left these items behind as some kind of twisted reminder that she was "still there". I can say with confidence that not one item of hers is in my new home.

The only good product of that failed marriage is my stepson. Otherwise, no reminders are necessary of that woman. Remember these "easy removal" processes: burn, shred, or throw away negative disposable items. By hanging on to these items, you are allowing someone other than yourself to mentally control your life, even if it is in a small way. I do not directly deal with my husband's ex-wife because she does not respect me or my husband. Instead of allowing her to ruin mine, she will have to ruin someone else's day. Do not spend time with anyone who mistreats you. Limit time spent with a person or people who lack respect for you based on who you are. They will attempt to drag you down into the miserable place where they exist. If you want to stay happy, surround yourself with those who bring you happiness and make you feel great about yourself. What do you need to put in your tool kit to keep running effectively and efficiently to reach your dreams and goals? You take along anything and anyone that helps you to build the strongest self possible. This can be as small as a good luck charm from a family member or friend, or that you found for yourself. Hold onto and place these items into your emergency self-esteem kit that uplifts your mood. When you suffer a personal loss or setback, these mementos will remind you of how much others think or have thought highly of you. It also reminds us of how each of us can make someone else's journey better, just by being their friend or family member, or because you were there to help them become fully functioning again. These self-esteem boosters are proof that you have accomplished a lot in life already. Nobody can take your good memories or achievements away from you.

This method of replenishing your self-esteem will be meaningful for you and you may want to share your achievements with others close to you. When you feel down about yourself or your life, never forget the accomplishments and love you received from others when you were at your best. They are all still there cheering you on, even if it is from far away or a different way of being. They are still telling you, "Go ahead, you can do it. I know you can. I always believed that you could."

If you feel like you have a slow leak in your heart due to the loneliness or ridicule related to your self-esteem repair work, remember those silent supporters who are still pushing for you to succeed. They are smiling because they know your self-esteem will be working powerfully again, just like it did previously. You have forgotten or never knew how to protect yourself from damage to your self-esteem. If you carry the necessary tools in your tool kit, using the appropriate tool for each repair job, you can successfully overcome any obstacle in life.

*Chapter Five*

## Your Personal Crisis List for Major Disrepair

What are you going to do when you find yourself totally alone? (Believe me. You are going to have these times.) These will be some of the most difficult times you will ever experience. You may not know what to do. You may not have anyone to talk to. Remember that for any problem you may be struggling with, there is a person, support group, therapist, or crisis hotline that you can turn to. Call your local social service agencies for starters. The beauty of a crisis hotline is that you can choose to remain anonymous. Please call these trained professionals who can connect you with the tools you will need to fix yourself up into working order again. I can guarantee that you will create new relationships that can only improve your situation and social life. You will meet others in similar situations and develop friendships that may last a lifetime. You can never have too much support in a crisis.

A support group or professional that you meet with will help you to get rid of any excess weight on your spirit that is wearing you down. Once you figure out what is broken, you can detect it and find what you will need to repair yourself. Most of the time, you will already possess the tools for recovery from your crisis. For reasons that are only clear to you, you are not using the tools correctly or do not know which tools to use.

Think of your current or past job. What did you use to be effective at your job? Go step by step. Slow down and list the items that you need to be effective in your own life.

It is time to create your Crisis List.

Here are ten steps that can navigate you through a crisis:

1. Call a family member or friend who is emotionally available to you and a great listener, somebody who always stands by you.
2. Contact an agency or facility that helps people with your same situation to heal. Remember that for any physical, mental, or spiritual need there is an organization that can help you.
3. Write down who or what helped you deal with crises in the past.
4. Write down your attempts to overcome crises that have not worked.
5. Write down your weekly schedule, highlighting times when you are available to work on this issue.
6. Organize your work, family, and social time around the time required to address your crisis.
7. Write down things that you can do to safely make your situation better immediately, no matter how scary it may seem at this moment.
8. Take at least 24 hours (48 or more is even better) before you make a life-changing decision with careful consideration of your loved ones. Note: Do not let anyone rush you into making a decision that you are unprepared for. However, if your safety, possibly even your life, is at risk (or you have a premonitory gut feeling) then get out of there! Go to your local law enforcement agency for a safe haven in which you can make any necessary accommodations to keep you and yours safe.
9. Do what trained professionals advise to remain safe and sane. You are the only person who can choose to get yourself completely out of this crisis and back in working order, no one else can do it for you.
10. Whenever possible, remember to someday thank each person who helped repair you when you were broken. A simple "Thank you" note or card mentioning how he or she helped you in your repair work is sufficient and will give you closure.

Keep this Crisis List with you at all times with names, numbers, and addresses on it in case of an emergency. Find a pocket, wallet, or purse to carry your Crisis List with you. It will help you overcome any upcoming repair work or breakdowns, no matter how big or small they are.

Don't you feel stronger now that you have effective tools in that personal tool kit? You are functioning better now and getting closer to living your dreams and attaining your life goals.

## Chapter Six

Get out the hammer and chisel.
You have serious corrosion and it shows!

No man or woman is merely a sum of his or her parts, but it helps when your parts are all working properly and look the way you want them to. You need to be satisfied with your own physical appearance and that of your home. First, let's discuss your needs in the aesthetic arena. In these days of health consciousness there is no excuse for not taking excellent care of yourself. If your aesthetic issues require professional help, then find people who do the type of work that you need done. One example is to go to a dermatologist for facial discoloration or areas of concern. You can also try homeopathic remedies for your aesthetic needs. I know I look and feel a lot better when I have rejuvenation services done whether massage therapy or a complete head to toe overhaul. Go to your public library and see what you can use at home to exfoliate and refresh tired or discolored skin. Although I am not recommending it, you may require special equipment and machinery to get you to the self you would like to be. A plastic surgeon may be able to help you temporarily or permanently rid you of your perceived physical flaws.
If it is your appearance or physique that is troubling you, there is now a specialist, procedure, cream, or pill that can help you with

all of that. Also, if you are a person in good health with moderate financial means or the ability to save money for a rainy day or to be an outpatient, cosmetic surgery may be an excellent option for you. Otherwise, find an image consultant or stylist who, for a small fee, will tell you how to best utilize what you were born with. You will feel better in your own skin once you are striving to look and feel your best. If you cannot afford a gym, try walking, jogging, exercise DVDs, or alternative exercise programs such as yoga or Tai chi. Improve yourself as much as you personally desire so that you can be happy with your appearance. If you do not like yourself, you will never be able to help others or live to your potential because negative self-image lowers your energy levels and darkens other areas of your life with a self-loathing that can be disastrous.

You do not need to pay for the privilege to briskly walk around your neighborhood six, or even seven, days per week for 30 minutes to an hour. Also, you can use water bottles filled with sand or water for hand weights if you cannot access store-bought weights. You can consult with a fashion or style expert for a small fee who will show you what colors and styles look best on you. I have done this and it was an eye-opener even though I consider myself quite fashion savvy. Sometimes you just need one or more extra pairs of eyes to tell you what you are doing well (and not so well) to optimize your physical appearance. You only get one chance to make a first impression; therefore you had better make it dazzling rather than run of the mill.

Be a revivalist. Don't ever accept the cop-out that aging includes letting your body implode from misuse and having your face dry up and crumble off. It is unnecessary, self-defeating and, in all honestly, not very pleasing to the human eye. God gave you life. Live your life while striving to be your best self. You may not be able to stop wrinkles from forming, but you can minimize their impact with a little tender loving care and really good facial cream. Shine both inward and outward. If all else fails, the rumored Fountain of Youth is supposed to be located somewhere in Bimini, the Bahamian island forty nautical miles from Miami and St. Augustine, Florida. When you find it, let me know.

Remember those McCall's patterns that your Mom put away during the prime of the feminist movement when it was too "hausfrau" for a woman to actually sit in her home long enough to sew her own clothing on the *gasp* sewing machine? Here's another shock for your system: even I own a sewing machine. It is a great way to make custom clothing, drapes, tablecloths, etc., especially in times of economic sluggishness, so that you can better spend your money elsewhere. Call me frugal, but saving money by sewing is not anti-feminist. Sewing is just plain practical. Borrow or buy a sewing machine. You will use it more than you thought you would. Learn how to do minor sewing jobs to save money on trips to the tailor or to save your favorite work shirt with the mystery tear on it. It is amazing what a needle and thread can do to save work clothes and casual wear. If you cannot sew, take a class or ask a friend or family member who does sew to show you the basics. After you learn some sewing basics, you can frugally "DIY" your minor sewing projects.

Is your apartment or home looking run-down? Get help! Even if you are low on extra cash or have no extra cash for buying new furniture you can rearrange what you have. You can go to a local thrift store to find matching furniture that will cost you close to nothing. Check your local place of worship or consignment stores to see if your financial situation qualifies you for free items of furniture. It is better to have a donated bed and television stand than none at all (which can present an unnecessary health hazard to you and your loved ones). Safety and your health are more important than stubborn pride.

Depression-era men and women did fine without a penny in the bank account by turning to friends and neighbors to trade items back and forth. It is always better to ask for help, so do it. Who knows? Your friend may want to evenly trade their living room furniture for yours. Check yard sales. Someone may give you a sofa, chair, or other item for free. Stranger things have happened. Sometimes the kindness of a stranger is the most gratifying and most helpful because we know we will return the favor by helping someone else someday. I have heard of websites that are helping users obtain free items from other site group users living within close proximity to each other.

Now is the time that you may need help, so take it. Just remember to help someone else in a similar situation in the future. Not only should you do so, but it cleanses the soul and renews your spirit to help others in need. We have all had times when we needed help. Someone somewhere will be able to use your help when you are at your strongest. I have found this fact to be very true personally. I enjoy putting smiles on people's faces. Too many of us live in misery. We must work to lift each other up out of unhappiness. By helping another person to identify a problem similar to the one you once had, you can help this person to begin the work of repairing him or herself. Try not to feel badly when a person refuses your help. Some men and women do not want to be helped when you offer it. They may accept your help at a later date. Having an offer of help to helped refused is a difficult fact to wrap your head around, but you will have to honor that person's wish.

One of the hardest realities of social work to digest, which never got easier, was was when someone refused help, especially help that could have have positively impacted that person's life. Some people prefer to keep doing the same things that bring them misery because they are used to this level of existence. If you do not know anything better, you may not believe that there could be a better way of doing things.

If you refuse to let others teach you what they know, you may never find the best way to get things done. Acquiring the correct tools for the best life imaginable is crucial to your success. Gaining knowledge from others is essential to true happiness. Knowledge is a tool to rid your life of ignorance which can lead to disastrous situations. For example, if you are sick and refuse to go to the doctor, you could become terminally ill from a curable disease. On the other hand, with early detection and knowledge gained about the disease, you could hopefully get rid of it soon after it appears in your system, before it consumes your life. You can cause yourself and others a lot of unnecessary pain and suffering by neglecting your health. Let's suppose that your car is unsafe, impractical, or simply not your style. Try to replace it with another automobile, motorcycle, or other alternate transportation method. You may be amazed to find folks who would like to sell a car more than just make a large profit. The more you search, the more likely you are to find what you are looking for. Non-profit agencies assist young parents, unemployed workers, or low income men and women to acquire vehicles because without one they may not be able to find or hold down a job.

Go to a home improvement store that keeps throw-away exterior and interior home paint for resale. It will be deeply-discounted and you may just get enough resale paint to paint your entire home interior without having to buy a lot of cans at the full retail price. Ask friends, family, and neighbors if they have excess paint that they would like to get rid of. You may get your whole house or apartment repainted for free. An important fact in life is that you will not get a thing unless you ask for it.

If the local or national economy is in bad shape, frivolous spending is out of the question. It is urgent that you remain sensible about the improvements you make for yourself physically and for your living space. Do whatever you can within reason and that fits your particular budget. There are fabric stores, home improvement and consignment stores that will practically give certain products away for almost no cost to you. Do not be too proud to ask for the most economical product. Even the wealthiest among us like to be thrifty, so nobody is going to assume that you can't pay full price. If a sales associate is rude to you, you can always shop elsewhere. Enjoy your bargain hunting. I always do. I buy items at the antique shops that would cost you sometimes triple at a furniture store and they are often built better than many of today's products. You can make an older item new again with a little cleaning, creativity, and tender loving care. Besides, antiquing is considered an activity of the "well-to-do" which you know you are, so go ahead and "do-it-well."

Be happy and enjoy the relief you feel as you let go of past junk parts, those mementos that indicate terrible episodes of your life. Letting go of this junk will help you get over those junky situations mentally. De-clutter your living space of all things that, upon seeing them, make you feel inadequate or insecure. You are better off without that painful garbage. Holding on to these things is like keeping spare parts to a car that you don't own. What good are they?

Fill your living space with pleasant mementos. Put some on display throughout your home. Every time that you are feeling shaken up and need to recharge your spirit, you can physically see all that you have done successfully in happier times. Have an "I love me" wall or room in your home that is dedicated to only the things, people, or occasions that made you feel like a success when things were running smoothly. This decorating strategy helps you to feel better instantly upon viewing your decor. A driver in control of the vehicle of life is going to be a much happier one.

Think back to the happiest times in your life and how good you felt at those times. Try to think of what it was that gave you great joy and feelings of accomplishment. Those thoughts should make you feel better. That is exactly the point that I am trying to make. You must surround yourself with people and things that make you feel worthwhile in a way that is healthy for you. When you do this, you will gain the personal strength to carry on. You will have the correct tools and knowledge of how to use them to achieve your life goals one step at a time and one success at a time.

*er Seven*

My battery is dead.

Has anyone seen my jumper cables?

You will have future success as you fine-tune your life using the proper tools for each life event. Your life should be working a lot better once your self-esteem is working well and you've thrown the "I can't do it" thoughts out of your set of coping tools for your personal tool kit. The next steps to getting your personal happiness back on track will seem less cumbersome and much more likely to happen. You may feel as though all of the elements are working against you, that none of the things that worked in the past are working for you in the present. These are the times in life when you must be a completely selfish person, focusing on all of the situations in your world that you possess the tools to control. Is there an activity that made you feel great about yourself and made you feel worthwhile?

As long as an activity is healthy and legal, please do it as often as possible. This is your happiness we are talking about. If money is an issue, then choose a favorite activity that costs you little-to-nothing financially. Examples of cost-free activities are: enjoying a fitness walk or hiking along a scenic trail. You can also listen to your favorite song. Select songs that best allow you to deal with your situational emotions. What makes you feel the best when you are angry, frustrated with work or family matters, feeling anxious, or any other emotion that has short-circuited your self-esteem? Find that song. Find a relaxing activity. Face the music and unwind, allowing the raw emotions that you are feeling to work their way through, and then out of, your system.

Get those feelings of inadequacy out of your mind, or else your batteries will go dead in a living emotional nightmare that I wouldn't wish on anyone. Record these favorite songs or put the lyrics into your Emergency Self-Esteem Box. Make a list of healthy, legal activities that make you feel like the fantabulous person that you are.

Keep a copy of a memento that makes you feel happy and take it with you when you are away from home. If you feel like you have taken all that you can humanly stand emotionally, physically, or both, go take a look at your memento. Try to recall the feelings of happiness that your memory brings to the surface from a photo, note, or event. You feel better immediately, don't you? Just looking at it or holding it gives you an instant charge to get you through a difficult time. I carry a photo of my spouse and children as well as a childhood photo of my best friend and me for this reason.

I anticipate low energy times in life when I will experience distress. These photos, my mementos, help me to maintain my bearings and keep me strong. As I have said already, carry your tools for life's positives and negatives so that you are ready for those times when your battery needs charging. You will be prepared for anything that comes your way once you have tools in place to alleviate turmoil in your home and at your job. Use these tools when dealing with family, friends, and colleagues. You must make plans to take care of yourself outside of your responsibilities to others in your day-to-day life. Create a realistic and effective plan for renewing your energy and making sure that every part of yourself is in operating condition before you completely lose yourself (which is a disastrous situation for anyone).

*Chapter Eight*

## Substandard thoughts create self-doubt and accidents.

Have you ever thought to yourself or said aloud, "I'm losing it!" Well, you are losing "it." "It" is the control that you are losing over yourself and your life. You must recognize what or who is making you feel this helpless and out of control. Identify this thing or person or you cannot repair what is broken in your life. When dealing with a person who is making you feel like you are going to "lose it," let that person know as soon as they make the offense, not afterward when you can only think that you could have and should have brought it up. Do not bottle up your discontent. I follow this rule and men and women seem shocked and sometimes offended when I tell them they are being rude or that I do not appreciate their, or their child's, behavior. Trust me, you will not be carrying as much negativity around with you if you do it.

Being honest with yourself and others is very cathartic. Not putting up with people's nonsense feels really good. Nonsense that directly targets you must be dealt with immediately. Do not let the behavior whittle away your confidence to a nub. Do not accept other's bad behavior as something you should put up with. Clean that broken coping mechanism of allowing others to mistreat you out of your tool kit!

Is this process of ridding self-doubt from your mind going to always make you friends? No. Is it going to save you a lot of unnecessary heartache and pent up anger? You bet it will! There is such a thing as not being honest enough. Do not worry about being too honest with someone. Being painfully, but not cruelly, honest may lose you a friend. In all reality, if you have to pretend about who you are and what you stand for the entire time that you are around a certain individual, this person is not a true friend to begin with. This person probably never was a true friend. This kind of tool kit cleaning out of negative parts of your life that aren't working prepares you for the true friends who will like and respect the real you unconditionally. Stay away from people who enjoy frazzling you. Be aware of who likes to watch you overheat by creating conflict with you for no apparent reason. Limit or eliminate contact with anyone who puts you in a rapidly-moving deep downward spiral after which you require complete decompression to revive your one surviving last nerve.

For example, a co-worker asks you if you have "had something done," because you look so good. That's what my mother refers to as a backhanded compliment. It is meant to catch you off-guard and make you feel badly. The worst part is that the offender may not realize that he or she is having this effect on you. It is your job to explain why the comment bothers you or to devise a comeback comment that is a friendly acknowledgement of their ignorance to reverse the intended injury to you. In this example you can say something such as, "Thank you. I am just being myself. Thanks for noticing," giving the person the most cheerful smile that you can conjure up.

This kind of self-esteem boosting comeback is something that can take years of practice. Hopefully you will not have to be on the defense the majority of the time. This leads me to others who behave aggressively toward you or treat you punitively in a very specific way. You need to ask them why, no matter how difficult the answer may be for you to hear. Make sure that there is not a physical threat if you do so and make sure that you have another job lined up if this is a terrible work situation before you unload the emotional sludge that this person has been heaping on you. If you do get fired because you would not be victimized verbally or physically by a co-worker or supervisor, it is a blessing in disguise. You will hopefully never have to deal with this person again. You are probably wondering, "How is losing my job a good thing?" It is good to know that you will no longer be this human wrecking ball's favored target. You must call the shots, not continually put up with degrading comments or actions that put your self-esteem at risk. I remember, during my college years, being let go by a ferry company because, in my supervisor's opinion I could not type or do "mental math" quickly enough. My co-worker resorted to name calling. She even accused me of costing the company money because their business was dependent on the passengers filling each ferry.

Although the barrage of insults were untrue and bizarre, I knew I should pick up more hours at the grocery store that I had worked at as my primary job during the college year. I was happy to leave that maritime Hell on Earth located at Judith Point, Rhode Island. In that situation it was far better to be a passenger than an employee of the ferry company.

## Chapter Nine

## Help, I think I have a screw loose!
## How I survived sudden illness.

Your life has shattered into millions of tiny little pieces and you don't know how to put them back together. You are unsure whether or not the life you have known will ever look the same again. That is fine. Your life is never going to look the same again. Why would you want it to stay the same, anyway? Pick up the salvageable pieces and put your life back together bit by bit. Your life will be in fine working condition after you have chosen adhesive that is beneficial to your overall well-being, your spirit, and your self-esteem. Believe it or not, in my early twenties my life was shattered into fragments so tiny that I could barely see them to pick them up. I needed to find a magnifying glass to carefully examine what caused my life to disintegrate so quickly.

It was the Christmas Eve rush of 1995. A horde of customers needed their huge hams, giant turkeys, and tons of fixings to prepare their holiday dinners. As a cashier manager, I was running back and forth to the meat department toting hams and turkeys for those who couldn't, taking over for the cashiers when they needed their breaks, and quickly dealing with any customer service department crises. All of a sudden, I noticed that I was having difficulty lifting gallons of milk or other heavy items needing to be rung up and bagged.

It was as though my right hand and arm were so worn out that they had given up, saying to me, "You'd better use your left hand and arm because we are of no use to you today." My self-drawn conclusion was that I had pinched a nerve causing numbness and weakness in my hand and arm. Shortly afterward, I took my lunch break. I sat down at one of the break tables and began to eat. When I lifted my food to my mouth, it was as if the food had a hard time getting to its target. My arm felt heavy and my hand had gone almost completely numb. My co-worker said, "Looks like you pinched a nerve. You better be careful today, especially when you are lifting anything. Make sure you keep your back straight and bend your knees."

The advice that my co-worker gave me in the break room meant a lot to me because it eased my mind for the time being. I went back to my shift with a rubbery-feeling hand and an arm that was so heavy that it felt like lead. The next cashier had to be relieved, so I jumped onto the register. The going was slow for me. I had to use my left arm for any lifting since my right arm was useless. As I counted change back, I slurred like someone who had had too many drinks on dollar night at the local neighborhood bar. I immediately began to lose my composure. Was this voice coming from my mouth? Why was one side of my face not working properly?

A middle-aged customer said, "I have a sister who gets this. It's called Bell's palsy. It will go away on its own, but the cold weather and stress can trigger it." I largely ignored the comment and rang up a few more customers when my leg began to feel non-human. My leg was like rubber, really hard and as though it wasn't properly attached to my body. It was heavy, like someone had poured quick concrete around it, so heavy that I had to drag it with my body strength, scuffing the sole of my shoe to walk one foot in front of the other. It was difficult for me to walk properly and to keep my balance.

At this point I was beginning to get scared. Pins and needles could be a pinched nerve, but rubber and extreme heaviness had never been felt before in any of my limbs. The last straw came shortly afterward. While counting change back to a customer, she said, "You just gave me fifty-seven dollars instead of fifty-seven cents. You had better take a rest young lady." A good sob was working its way up through my body; however any crying jag would have to wait.

My entire right side was numb. The pins and needles left and a cold other-worldly paralysis had taken its place. Immediately I thought to myself, "*This must be a heart attack. I'm losing my ability to think clearly. I feel light-headed.*" I had never felt this disconnected from my body before. It was time to call 9-1-1. My manager, Kevin, was paged to the front office. In the safety of the office, the anxious tears found their way to the surface of my half-frozen face. I wiped them with the hand that still seemed to have life in it. I explained my symptoms to Kevin and he said, "I am not calling 9-1-1. If you are just trying to get out of working today, then pack your things and Merry Christmas. Do you have any idea how many employees, especially on a holiday, say they are deathly ill and have to go home? You look fine Lara. Personally, I think you should get back to your shift. I need you here, period," he said this with so much lack of concern and distrustfulness that I became furious.

I responded, "Well, Kevin, let me tell you that if you do not call 9-1-1, that I may die from whatever is making my right side heavy and useless. Will that make you happy? Do you want to see me pass out, because I feel like I could? I probably shouldn't drive. Please pick up the phone and call an ambulance before I collapse." Kevin knew I was deadly serious, but had a paralysis of his own to deal with, a huge mental management paralysis called "denial."

I told him that I had to go because I was afraid of what might happen next. My right leg was so heavy and stiff that I had to drag it alongside my working left one. Anyone looking at me must have determined that I was either out of my mind or that I had a prosthetic leg that had me possessed. Either way, it didn't matter. Nobody and nothing could stop me from what I had to do. My job now was to get myself to South County Hospital, the closest to the store, before the light-headedness caused me to lose consciousness. I felt like I didn't have any time to waste.

I do not remember anything from the drive. My last alert memory was as I sat in a wheelchair in the Emergency Room Waiting area. The nurse had tears in her eyes and said firmly and loudly, "This poor girl is having a stroke or something and is in really bad shape." My whole body seemed to be shutting down. My strength to walk was missing. The doctors and nurses quickly wheeled me to a trauma room curtain stall and helped me undress. I remember an ER technician showing me my things, promising to lock my belongings up until my family showed up. I could barely speak to thank him.

One of the young ER doctors was confused by my age and symptoms, so he grabbed an older doctor. The older, bearded and white-haired doc said, "That young woman is stroking out." Then I heard him shout to whoever was helping, "Get the Heparin and a pain killer, yesterday, before she crashes." *A stroke?* I had quit my late night college partying months earlier, worked hard my whole adult life, was in great shape, and only twenty-three years old. He must be talking about some other young lady.

Strokes kill people. Strokes are for eighty-year-olds, not young people like me. The young doctor came in with an ER nurse to administer Heparin and a pain killer called Demerol. Just then, Mom and Dad showed up. I was so happy to see them. They rushed to hug and kiss me with Mom saying, "We will be right back, your brother was behind us and we want to tell him what to expect before he gets back here. OK, Lara?" This wasn't sounding so hot. *Prepare Liam? For what!? Was I dying or something? Why wasn't anybody saying anything to me?*

Dying is kind of a serious thing. Why was it that nobody could gather the nerve to tell me, the person potentially ready to croak? Before my parents got to the hospital, a customer from the grocery store recognized me. She spoke to me, "I know you. You run the grocery store over there. Are you really sick?" I told her rather morbidly, "Yeah. They think it's a stroke or something. Nobody knows for sure. Thank you for caring enough to ask." She said, "You're welcome. I'll say a prayer for you to get better soon." I weakly thanked her with all of the false strength that I could pretend to exude. The lightheadedness was getting worse. I felt very cold. The numbness was rapidly spreading throughout my body. My parents filed in, first Mom, then Dad, and finally my red-faced, teary-eyed, visibly-distraught brother, Liam. Mom asked, " How are you feeling Lara?" I remember answering, "Like, you-know-what Mom, like I'm dead on one side. It is taking too much energy to talk right now." My brother had to leave the room because he started to break down. My mother rushed to get the doctors and nurses for some reason. Dad just started crying, something he never did.

I could hear my mother saying, "My daughter just passed out and her heart rate is slowing down." All of a sudden, I saw a bright, soft light above me. I felt ecstasy, pure joy. My body was gone. The only sensation that I had was my sight. The only feeling was of happiness, relief, a true sense of calm, and painlessness. I could see my parents below me at the foot of the gurney. All three were holding each other crying. My only frustration was that I could not audibly speak to them, but I kept trying to send them comforting thoughts.

This had to be Heaven because my problem was replaced by total contentment. I kept trying to send thoughts to them, *It's OK you guys. I am not in any pain. I am floating above you and I am so happy, with a deep happiness that I have never felt before. It feels so good. I wish I could speak to you or touch you to comfort you and to let you know that I am fine.* Then, the bright light that I had been wrapped in like a blanket began to lose its not-of–this-world brilliance. It began to turn yellowish. It was like the glow of a fluorescent light.

I could see a body under blankets and something flat and white above my feet. I heard strange adult voices saying things like, "She's waking up. Her eyes are opening." I couldn't speak. When I opened my mouth, no words came out. *Was I still dead? What was happening to me?* Then, I heard my mother. She said to me, "I knew that might work, the hanging upside-down trick." I vaguely felt sensation as my bed moved to a horizontal position from a bizarrely vertical one. Mom informed me that the doctors were sending me to Rhode Island Hospital in Providence to figure out what was wrong. She said, "We will see you up there tomorrow." I was too exhausted to bother asking why they weren't spending Christmas Eve with me. They said, "We'll follow the ambulance to see that you get there okay and then we have to get home as soon as you're situated."

Medical personnel filed into the ambulance along with two emergency medical technicians otherwise known as EMTs. They told me what to expect, that they would have sirens and lights on the entire trip to Rhode Island Hospital to get me there as quickly as possible. A thirty-something male EMT accompanied me with a female in the back of the ambulance. I felt myself losing consciousness again. The male EMT scolded, "Nobody's dying on my watch. You are going to stay awake Lara." He found a sharp needle-like instrument to poke my foot.

I couldn't feel it at all in my right foot, so he tried the bottom of my left foot. He held my hand the whole way to Providence and squeezed it hard every time I almost passed out. He constantly checked my vital signs and reassuringly said, "Hang in there. My buddy is going as fast as legally possible and people are getting out the way. We'll be there real soon. They have some of the best doctors in the state up there to get you fixed up." Then he grabbed me by my numb hand again, asking me if I could feel him squeeze my fingers.

I replied, "No. It just feels like rubber, just like the right side of my body does." Our journey to Rhode Island Hospital was ending. The EMTs went to find out where I was supposed to go to wait for a room. The lobby was freezing cold. My parents had followed the ambulance. I was glad that they had not abandoned me yet. I'm sure they were tired but I was possibly at death's door. The least they could do was to make sure I wasn't on my way through it. Hospital orderlies wheeled me away from the lobby where the EMTs had waited with me. I thanked the hard-charging EMTs for keeping me awake and getting me to the hospital so quickly. They all told me to get better soon and that I would know what's happening right away with all of the specialists available to me there.

I tried to smile with the side of my face that was still working. I sat in the hallway feeling very alone. My mother walked up to my gurney saying, "We'll see you tomorrow for Christmas once you are all situated here." I couldn't believe she and Dad were leaving when I was half paralyzed, seemingly close to death, and depressed that I was spending Christmas in a huge city hospital away from friends and family. I looked around at people in the corridor. In two of the seats on the left side of it were Jennifer and Leslie, two of my friends that I had grown up with in Charlestown. Jennifer was my closest friend since first grade and still is. Leslie grew up with us, dated my brother for a short time, and was so incredibly sweet for waiting with Jen to check on my progress. Jen had been crying. She tried to look tough with her back straight and smiled at me saying, " I know you like men to scramble wildly to take care of your every desire, but this is ridiculous!"

That's Jen. I was physically as weak as I had ever been, but she somehow made me laugh so hard that I could almost feel a full bladder. Jen explained that she couldn't celebrate with her family when she knew I was in a strange place, so sick that I couldn't feel my own body. She and Leslie were staying until I got a room and proper medical attention. Leslie said, "I've had my life fall apart before with my ex-husband, not knowing what tomorrow will bring. It scares you so bad that you can't think of anything else. Plus, Jen needs a friend with her because she is a wreck with worry about what's wrong with you. And frankly so am I." It felt so good knowing that Leslie and Jennifer were spending their Christmas

Eve with me when my parents, for whatever irrational reasons, could not.

Jen and Leslie told me funny jokes about some of the townies and any wild things they had done, about their holiday plans, and kept asking the doctors and nurses if my room was ready yet. It must have been very late at night but that hospital was like Grand Central Station, always clogged with sickies like me waiting to live or die. I was determined to live, deciding that my next near-death experience could wait until I was at least one hundred years old, not twenty-three. God couldn't take me now. I was finally over my cheating ex-boyfriend, deep into my social work program at the University of Rhode Island, and seemed to have good control over every aspect of my life, except for one thing: my body.

Jennifer told me that a room was available on the Respiratory Ward. I would be in a four-patient room. Hopefully they were not all falling apart like I was. Why was I going to an acute respiratory ward? Were the doctors afraid that I would stop breathing? I didn't get it, any of it. Finally, I got my room assignment. It was a small step up from an ER treatment room, except with a window view of some rundown buildings, as decrepit looking as I was feeling.

I had roommates, all three of them. My college health insurance did not qualify me for the one-patient luxury suites on the other side of the hospital. One was 92 years old and looked like she was definitely nearing her last breath with monitors attached to her for every bodily function known to man. She sounded like she was Italian or Portuguese, speaking a mix of broken English and foreign tongues. At any given time, she had at least two of her family members praying over her or surrounding her bed.

The woman across from me was a homeless lady, about sixty years old according to her chart, who was a frequent tenant in the acute respiratory ward. She was constantly disgustingly flatulent, always with a yummy can of Ensure in her hand. The nursing staff had to wait for her to have a bowel movement before they could send her back to the freezing streets of Providence. Honestly, I couldn't wait until this immensely obese, malodorous discontent relieved herself and the rest of us of her brand of "holiday cheer." My nurse said, "She starves herself to get back to her self-created Club Med, then its off to the mean streets of Providence with her homeless buddies."

Last but not least was a thirty-ish Guatemalan woman with gorgeous huge brown eyes and a pretty smile. She looked like she had been in a bad accident with one side of her face severely swollen. She spoke only Spanish, but I used hand signs and my inadequate *espanol* to ask what the lump was on the side of her face. I discovered from the medical staff that it was an abscessed tooth that had ruptured, releasing dangerous bacteria into her bloodstream. The infection was wreaking havoc with her entire body, the poor woman. As though being a new immigrant was not difficult enough, her mouth decided to grow bacteria that could have been the end of her American Dream had she not been at the hospital getting antibiotics intravenously. Since she was the only one of three who was still an alert Earthling, I would find ways to communicate with my new *amiga*.

The first night in the hospital was a lonely, scary nightmarish scenario. I needed help going to the bathroom. I was too weak and off balance to go solo. Plus, my new dance partner, Mr. I. V. Pole, had to go everywhere with me. It was the first time, and hopefully the last, that I could not go to the bathroom from fatigue. Like the homeless queen, I too had some problems below the belt. I pulled the emergency help rope hanging next to the toilet. I was frantic because my body wouldn't do what I was willing it to. I was a blubbering, frustrated exhausted mess.

The kindest nurse showed up. She had long auburn hair, a wicked sense of humor, and true compassion. All three were things I was in desperate need of. I had not showered in two days and was beginning to smell pretty funky. I asked my stylish, high-spirited, red-haired nurse if I could get help cleaning myself for Christmas visitors. She told me that after her rounds, she would get a basin with fresh water to wash my hair and body. It was a major relief to me knowing that my friends, family, and some old dates of mine were coming to see me during visiting hours. Christmas Day was not the best since I was laid up, half-paralyzed in a respiratory ward with the lady in the corner coding about every few hours, the flatulent Ms. Malodorous, and my international "normal" roommate who had the best smile for someone whose infected tooth almost killed her. I had a steady flow of amazed mostly twenty-something medical interns, getting the chance of a lifetime to study the 23-year-old with the almost-fatal traveling blood clot with resulting residual paralysis on her right side. When I wasn't a spokesmodel for medical freaks of nature, I was visiting with close family and friends.

I had three phone calls from a guy that I dated in high school, one I currently dated in college, and one from my most recent ex-boyfriend, James, who I had been over for several months before my medical problem raised its ugly head. My mother actually called James to tell him about my medical disaster and he wanted to know if he could visit me the day after Christmas to wish me "a Merry Belated Christmas" as a "friend." I told him that it would be fine and what to expect. The young man I had been dating called and I told him that I did not want to see him at all. His name was Elliot, a very ego-driven pre-law guy with a chip on his shoulder the size of the North Pole, very icy, quite handsome, and very intelligent.

A man named Gary called, a high school friend of mine who summered in my hometown. He was now a meteorologist working in the Boston area. Gary said he had stopped at my parents' house to tell them he had finished meteorology school which took him the past six long years to complete. Like a dating Rip Van Winkle, he had decided that the forecast of being alone with a great degree wasn't so hot. My parents, acting as twisted social event planners told him to visit the day after Christmas, like James was. I told him that visiting later would be fine, since I knew James would be gone by noon. I would be finished with tests and interns by mid-afternoon.

I looked forward to seeing my old summer beach buddy, Gary, the perpetual flirt who always brought me a flower to my summer job, no matter where I worked. He always rode a moped when we turned 16 and he now had a BMW motorcycle, a much sexier ride. We had an excellent telephone conversation and I looked forward to seeing a person who had never directed an unkind word my way. I wondered what he looked like now. Thanks to my alleged blood clot, my memory was temporarily worthless. My sense of day and time was very off too. It didn't matter what day, month, or time it was. I was alive. That was all that mattered to me. My Christmas gift from God was miraculously getting my life back. The doctors and their pupils were constantly filtering in and out of my hospital room to inform me of tests that they would be conducting. The next day, I would have a CT scan in the morning and an MRI in the afternoon. James would be there in the morning. Gary would be there later in the day. I had one family member after another come in on Christmas day. That was one thing that my family was good at, showing up at weddings, funerals, and near-death exhibitions which sadly enough there have been several. Since I fit into the latter category, I was in constant company of one family member or another all Christmas Day long. The hospital food was festive, although I couldn't have any sodium until the risk for a recurring blood clot was gone. I couldn't drink my beloved coffee, either, which disturbed me because I definitely needed an energy boost of some kind to get me through the worst Christmas ever. The hospital is the last, most depressing, place I could ever be a patient in on the celebration of Christ's birth. We had Christmas music on the radio attached to the very old hospital bed. The ninety-or-so–year-old woman in the corner hadn't coded last night. She was going strong for Christmas. Ms. Malodorous was farting away rather contently hoping to never be regular again, since upon achieving a healthy BM she would be sent out into the cold once more. Even she had a visitor this holiday, a good-looking older, calm, soft-spoken gentleman in a sophisticated gray wool suit and fedora. He seemed rather smitten with my gassy roomie. He had a walrus mustache and small round-lensed thick glasses with watery, emotional eyes underneath them. She was lucky that he cared enough to stand by her side, but she was apparently emotionally unavailable to him.

My Guatemalan friend was visiting with her husband and older children. No young children were allowed due to possible airborne illnesses. I had no visitors yet; however I received a phone call from my Uncle Jeff, my Dad's old best friend from high school who was a Vietnam veteran like my father. He was a chosen family member, but a great one just the same. Uncle Jeff was up in the Providence area visiting his parents with his family. Uncle Jeff explained that he couldn't visit me with his wonderful, forward-thinking, holistic chiropractic physician wife because of the small children rule. I did not blame them, but they were missed.

Uncle Jeff was Dad's best friend in high school, volunteered for Vietnam like Dad did, and lived in a commune after the war in the 1970's. Uncle Jeff met his new wife in a communal setting, a beautiful young Methodist woman who had a heart of gold and Herculean convictions about the failing American healthcare system, even though they received specialized care at a hospital for their child who had serious respiratory problems. I love Uncle Jeff. He's a survivor like Dad, never failing to make life better each day. Uncle Jeff put his life back together, overcame addiction, a bad marriage, and the residual mental horrors left behind by his service in Vietnam, to completely rebuild his life.

Uncle Jeff and his new wife invited me down to their farm in Louisa County, Virginia, for spring break from my sophomore year of college. He and his wife Julia had three gorgeous children, a baby boy, a two-year-old girl, and the oldest was their four-year-old son. Their baby was medically vulnerable due to an inability to sweat. He had been medevacked several times in his all-of-six-months of age. Thank God Julia was a successful chiropractor. They had a beautiful multi-acre horse property in Louisa County. Louisa County, Virginia, was a quiet scenic place with a lot of equines and very friendly residents. Uncle Jeff taught me to ride a horse Western style during the week that I stayed with them. He had done electrical and carpentry work for Sissy Spacek who lived nearby. Uncle Jeff told me that she often spoke with the contractors offering them food and drinks when she was at the house.

They introduced me to all-natural medicine, food, and other household products which was an education for me. Uncle Jeff explained his journey of keeping his life from becoming cluttered by the past. He had the tools to maintain his mind, body, and family. He had become a full-time Dad which he said was the best job he ever had. Julia, Uncle Jeff's soul mate, was an incredibly strong woman and a complete Earth Mother who only used homeopathic medicine and organic food for her family all except for her baby's medical needs which required hospital care.

I had a beginning ear infection and she prescribed mullein ear oil. It cured my infection in only two days. This ear treatment is one that I have shared with anyone with fluid in their ears. It is truly a miracle oil. I was a vegan those precious unforgettable days that I spent at their homestead. Instead of sunburn, foolish men, and the usual spring break mayhem, I had found peace, healthy food, and new ways to take care of myself. I understood why Thomas Jefferson seldom left Monticello. The tranquility of the quaint towns and small cities of Virginia's backcountry are soothing to the senses.

Instead of coming to the hospital, Uncle Jeff invited my parents to have Christmas dinner with his family. Dad told me it was great to see Jeff doing so well with his new marriage, children, and peacefulness in his life. Dad remembered when Uncle Jeff was stuck in "prison" with a terrible marriage, overwhelming substance abuse, and jobs that went from bad to worse. Dad was thrilled to see the new and improved Uncle Jeff. I was told they chatted for hours that night. That report made me happy because they had always been so close, blood brothers until the end. My only living Grandfather, my Dad's dad, decided to stop by with a fruit and nut basket. It seemed very appropriate, the fruit symbolized my almost fruit-cake mentality and nuts symbolized how very nutty I could easily become if I allowed my new illness to ruin me. Jen, my lifelong best female friend, came in with cookies from Leslie's mother, Mrs. Connor, a former school aid when we were all in Elementary School. I didn't ask for anyone's permission. Not even the risk of death could keep me from a fresh-baked cookie while infirm at the hospital. The cookies were so delicious. I remember eating them very slowly to savor every morsel.

Jennifer stayed for a long time that Christmas day. We have been great friends since first grade when we would push each other out of our bus bench seats for fun. We respected each other's strength and determination when we were very young and still do. Jennifer is a forever friend. We have done a lot of the same things in life, just in different order. We lovingly refer to each other as "Bims" because we both get offended when some women pretend to be complete fools and dress scantily at inappropriate venues, i.e. preschool drop-off and pick-up. I have seen some mothers that could have been on their way to perform in a burlesque cabaret. That behavior is just wrong. That is not women's liberation. There are more appropriate instances for body baring, i.e. the beach or by the pool, but not dropping your toddler off to class. If a man behaved in the same way, he would be arrested for indecent exposure at the very least. The last classification type that we would ever want to be is the bimbo stereotype, so we jokingly call each other "Bim" to remind each other that we are much more than merely the sum or appearance of our parts. We take pride in being well-read and sensible.

No matter where in the world we have been geographically, Jen and I have always been there for each other. I carry a photo of Jen and me, a photo booth reel made when we were in tenth grade. We are laughing in that photo, two bimbaceous young women ready to take on the world. Every time that I experience an ungodly moment in life, I take that photo of Jen and me out of my purse, gaze upon it, and smile. In an instant, that horrible feeling disappears from my mind. Jennifer has the best sense of humor. She told me that I was not allowed to die until we could be old and grey with some grandkids to run after. I could not agree with her more, so I promised that I would try hard not to die again, emphasizing that God must have put me back here on Earth for a reason. She agreed. No more dying!

Jen knew more about death than most people did twice her age. Jen's Dad, a handsome, bandana-on-the-head wearing, motorcycle-riding free spirit, died when we were fifteen. I had been her only friend who met her father. Jen is a hardworking single mother who is always an inspiration to me. She is the sister that I chose for myself. I have a couple of "sisters" out there. They add a richness to my life that no dollar amount could match. We are always there for each other. Thank God for true friends who always think the best of each other and can be trusted in any situation. These friends are hard to find and some of my tools to maintain my strength on any occasion.

My best childhood friend, Jen, is intelligent, compassionate, tough, and has a sharp wit that can make me fall down in spasms of laughter. She has been my matron of honor and a lifelong confidante. She is a Portuguese powerhouse. I hope we will be Bingo-playing grandmas some day, laughing in the face of death, averting the aging process and death as well as the baby boomers seem to. Jen's house was a second home to many of us "townie" children as she was an only child which was an uncommon occurrence in small town Middle America. Kate, Jen's mother, is a very open-minded, hardworking woman who always did well without a second spousal income ,whose parents lived with her as they got older. Now Jen's mother has grandchildren in her home and is a wonderful grandmother as well. If I needed good sound advice from a very strong woman besides my own mother, Kate was a trustworthy wise sage. She could always be counted on for her feminist pearls of wisdom that were helpful in keeping strong young women like ourselves on track.

Another of my childhood friends who I will refer to as
Heather, would be acquainted with death in the not-so-distant future in a domestic violence attack by an ex-boyfriend. He told her on the day that she stopped dating him, "If I can't have you, than nobody can." She went to the police but since he had no previous record they could not put a restraining order on a person who had never harmed her physically. A few days later, he decided to try to end her life with a gun and ended up killing himself instead, while leaving her in a coma. She should never have had to go through any of that horror. I thank God and modern medicine that she survived. God forgive me, I do not feel badly for the deceased ex-boyfriend. Mentally ill or not, nobody has the right to take somebody else's life. I hope she will tell her story someday to domestic violence victims because they need to know that they are not alone, but that is up to her, not me. It is too painful for me to recount, so I can only imagine what she still feels about the incident.

Remember the crisis list advice from Chapter Five: to leave if your life is threatened. The individual just may be unstable enough to follow through with the threat. Get professional help from law enforcement, mental health professionals, friends and family, whoever and whatever it takes to keep you safe. You will make it to a better place in life. Others will show you better tools to use for healthy relationships so that you do not have to return to an abuser. You can do it. You are stronger than you give yourself credit for.

The two worst kinds of individuals to visit anyone in the hospital when she feels like one side of her body is dead are lovesick meteorologists and exes. Into my hospital room walked James in the peach-colored shirt and gold tie that I had bought him as a Valentine's Day gift the year before. James was a very attractive Italian-Irish man whose only hang-up was that he was studying a foreign-born damsel in distress instead of college writing at Rhode

Island College. He wanted a main course of my companionship with side dish of seductive single mother. Let's just say it ended badly. The two types of people I least like are liars and cheats. He suddenly fit into both categories. I didn't know if I wanted to kiss him or strike him over the head with my outdated bedside telephone. Oh, James was the total dreamer, "I am going to be a big Hollywood director like Matt Damon someday," he would say on almost a daily basis. He visited me for a while; long enough to tell me he and his exotic flavor-of-the-semester were caput. What did he expect me to say? I surely did not blame the object of his transgression. I blamed James for cheating when he knew that I loved him enough to marry him and that I would never do what he had done to me. After we were done catching up, a CT scan technician came into the room to rescue me from an incredibly strange situation with James. The truth is that I was excited to see James again. He held my hand all the way to the CT scan room, constantly apologizing for hurting me the way he had, how he lied, and how he was miserable over how badly he had hurt me. Temporarily, I forgave him.

James explained that he would visit me at my parents' house as much as I would allow him to. He leaned over to kiss me on the lips. I turned my cheek to him. The break-up emotions were still too raw, plus he had been on loan to another woman only half a year earlier. The CT scan tech said, "That boy really loves you doesn't he?" I answered, "Yes he does. I'll always love him too. I just don't know if we can ever be together again like we used to be. Anyway, it was great to see him." After my CT scan, I had family and friends waiting to see me in my room. My very cool Aunt Mary, one of my Dad's sisters, was there with my cousin Tom, her son. She is perpetually single, vowing to never marry again. She has perfectly silver hair, the figure of a twenty-year-old, and refuses to act her age. It is wonderful. I hope that I age as well. I plan to never age gracefully. You are only as old as you allow yourself to be. Defying time by trying to look and feel younger is how I deal with aging. As I have known for a long time, your mental and physical ages can be very different. Age is just a number. How you feel in general is more important than age.

My cousin Tom has a great sense of humor like his mother. He sympathetically commented, "Sorry that you have to spend Christmas in this place." I said rather sarcastically, "It's alright. I have a holiday dinner coming and I'm not alone. It's just me and Transvestite Timmy tonight. We'll have a blast!" Then, everyone began to laugh. The nurses had brought in a tissue paper and cardboard figurine for my hospital tray that looked like a Dickensian blonde version of Tiny Tim's head with a green tissue bell-shaped bottom that looked like an evening gown, thus the transvestite analogy. I mean no offense to anyone with cross-dressing tendencies. I direct the gender confusion only to the flimsy paper doll. I have an immense respect for both cross-dressing men and women. Some men have much better figures than I could ever dream of having and make much prettier women than they do men. I have seen beautiful performers in drag who were such wonderful singers. This world would be a much better place if we would all accept men and women for who they truly are instead of being hateful by insulting or trying to change them. All things considered, Tiny Tim and I decided that we would never spend Christmas in a hospital again.

The following day, a psychiatrist came into the room with a handful of Ivy League medical interns asking my permission to "examine" me. Mind you, I am not a huge fan of psychiatrists, as my mental health ideology runs along more of a non-medical holistic human services one. Psychiatrists, on the other hand, assume their patients are sick and must be medicated in order to get well. Some people need medication but studies in recent years show that some need more communicating and less pills to have a healthy state of mind. I have met some very odd psychiatrists. Some have been chain smokers, some were swingers, and some with almost non-human demeanors with a calculated condescending tone toward their patients. This chap was definitely one of the insensitive doctors, a *One Flew Over the Cuckoo's Nest* type who proved himself to be quite an ice cold torture device.

The psychiatrist asked me ridiculous questions like, "Has stress in your life ever caused you to be numb on one side or to possibly exaggerate your symptoms?" After answering him in the negative, he asked me to stand up. This seemed to be a weird request of someone who had decreased sensation and strength on one side from a suspected traveling blood clot. I humored this ringmaster of insanity by standing up, sticking my chest out, and declaring, "See? I am able to stand up just fine. I am a little tired from a blood clot and all of the hospital noise. There is a lady over there who could code any second, my homeless friend across the way is drunk on Ensure, and my Guatemalan girlfriend has a lethally-infected tooth." I was getting tired of his foolish questions. I decided to tell him that perhaps he should focus his attentions on the mentally ill rather than the physically-distressed. Then he continued his inquisition, "Could you jump on one leg, first on your good leg, then on your bad one?" Now I was really irritated, but I hopped pogo style for him, with my chest aching as I was bra-less in my fabulous hospital couture. He concluded, "You did that very well. I think you will be just fine in time." I asked him if he was finished with the twenty questions because I would rather be alone. He started going on and on about how keeping my feelings bottled up could cause emotional problems. That was the last straw. First he accused me of faking residual paralysis from a blood clot. Then, he had me doing low impact aerobic activity without even a sports bra. Finally, he decided that it was time for a little personality test to see if my medical condition was making me crazy. It was time for some healthy venting. I ordered, "Take yourself and your shrinks-in-training out of my room because if you stay here bothering me for one more second, although I am not insane, you'll push me to it. Get out of here and don't come back. Thank you, doctor." He left rather miffed. I didn't prove to be a good psychiatric guinea pig.

Following that weird science, I had a fun-filled spinal tap

scheduled. A middle-aged doctor came in, short white hair and brown-rimmed glasses over frosty blue eyes, accompanied by a young man, another intern from Brown University, who resembled a young JFK, Jr. He warned me, "This is my first spinal tap on a living subject, so I apologize if you suffer a spinal headache after I perform the test." That made me feel confident about the procedure. The doctors had to test for multiple sclerosis since some of my symptoms were characteristic of the disease. I didn't care what they had to test me for as long as they found out what wasn't working that got me there to begin with.

An old high school buddy, Julie, brought me a Dunkin' Donuts coffee, also not on the Rhode Island hospital menu, that I had to sip through a straw since I was lying flat for the day after the spinal tap procedure. I drank it with a strong conviction as I allowed the vigorously-craved caffeine to course through my veins. She was a nursing student and checked all of the pages of my chart to try to figure out what they had concluded so far about my mystery illness.

The nurses and phlebotomists had used every common available vein for IV meds, dye imaging, and let's not forget the endless blood work. The phlebotomist on shift, a big, brawny red headed twenty-something young man with a crew cut said, "I am sorry, Lara, but I have orders to take blood and the only veins that aren't blown are in your foot." That was when I went from exhausted respiratory patient to superfreak in about three seconds flat. I said with an authoritative tone, "Tell your supervisor that I am refusing all further blood testing until there is a vein in my upper body that can handle it. I am not a human pin cushion or lab rat for the students in this hospital. Let the Powers That Be know how I feel." After he left, I remained lying flat because of the previous spinal test and cried bitterly.

None of this was fair. Yes, I was happy to be alive. I was only twenty-three years old with my whole life ahead of me. Why did my body decide to short circuit? I had my phone back after intentionally dropping it the day before when the man I was dating said he couldn't make it to see me with all of his social commitments during the holidays. I would never speak to him again. One of his roommates soaped his entire car when I told her what he had pulled ,which gave me some satisfaction no matter how devious the activity had been. I later found out that he was a mental disaster, a chronic liar, and an extremely poor student. He was definitely not my type. Rule number one for a social work student is to never get involved with someone who is believed to have serious emotional issues. I have always lived by this rule since that episode.

Working in mental health is extremely rewarding. However, you are working to help others put the pieces of their lives together. The last thing you should do is to have a relationship with someone who is draining your energy with his or her emotional problems. This is self-destructive and will ultimately diminish your effectiveness at your social work job. It is your responsibility to help your clients, but not somebody you are dating. After we parted ways, his doctor called my apartment looking for him. I asked if I was in danger. The doctor said that he had missed appointments and wasn't taking his medicine. Thank God for patient confidentiality laws, because I didn't want to know the rest. I had my locks and my phone number changed immediately after that phone call.

The last thing I needed was a mentally-unstable date to make an unwanted visit. That is the fodder for a teen horror movie that I wasn't willing to star in. I saw him years later at my hometown's very compact grocery store, the Mini Super. He just stared at me without saying a word. I am happy that he got to see how strong and well put together I was since those days after my almost fatal sudden illness while a student at the University of Rhode Island. Once people who used to wear you down emotionally see you strong again, they are speechless. Do not expect them to be happy for you. Most likely you are looking at the same miserable, mixed-up person you knew years before. Most adult tigers don't change their stripes. They just accessorize differently and drive someone else to the land of all things outrageous instead of you.

*Chapter Ten*

*Where is that duct tape?*
*The Scotch tape holding my life*
*together isn't working.*

I was discharged after five long days of being poked and prodded in every way possible. The elderly woman was taken from the room while I slept. My homeless buddy was back on the streets probably dreaming of a warm hospital bed and Ensure smoothies. My Guatemalan friend was still fighting her infection while she awaited oral surgery. She was a wonderful woman, wife, and mother. We spoke a lot as I used my pocket translator to gab with her. I wish I could find her to thank her for her companionship and kind words during those dark days. It was off to my parents' house to convalesce and plan how to deal with my illness. Deciding not to go back to the grocery store, I took a job at a group home agency. I just couldn't work for a person who did not value an employee's life enough to dial 9-1-1. It was time to work in my chosen field of social work.

    I wanted to get some mental health experience under my belt. Less than a year went by and I was back in my own apartment in Westerly, Rhode Island. The apartment was the third floor of a gorgeous slate blue ornate Victorian with white gingerbread trim and a huge front porch. My apartment had once been the servants' quarters and house kitchen. I liked the huge kitchen. The doors leading in and out of the kitchen were intact, so it wasn't difficult to imagine the servants cold from the winter drafts and blazing hot in the summer. That apartment had the draftiest walls and windows I had ever experienced other than in an army tent. The old wood floors creaked as though they could give way at any moment.

I had to pay cash for my medical follow-up and was quickly running out of money for food and hygiene products. I needed a roommate and luckily a friend of mine agreed to rent the second bedroom. Now that my rent and utility bills were cut in half, my quality of life improved. My roommate was a kind person, never late with the rent, and emotionally supportive. I was thrilled to be getting stability back in my life. I could once again afford newspaper delivery and could enjoy going out with my friends. I began dating a kind, handsome young man that I met at Misquamicutt Beach who lived in Montreal. Dan was French-Canadian, so we spoke to each other *en francais* and got along famously. Montreal is a close second to Paris, France. The city is clean, fashionable, and vibrant with its European-like closeknit neighborhoods and omnipresent air of romance. Dan was an excellent cook, a great dancer, *tres romantique*, family-oriented, and hard-working. He was a purchaser for the Canadian version of Home Depot. Dan was stylish, well-raised, and very cultured with a huge reproduction of Monet's "Water Lilies" on his townhouse wall. He was a class act. We went on the ski lift up Mont Tremblant in the summer and walked together through Mount Royal Park at summer's end vowing to keep in touch regardless of our busy schedules.

It was back to the fall semester of 1996. I was on my way to a class in the animal science building when I lost feeling in my right hand and arm. This numbness was worse than the previous winter's. I knew I was in trouble. I became disoriented and began to quietly weep as I felt so weak that I had to sit down on one of the plastic chairs in the lobby of the building. After gaining some self-control, I decided to skip class and get back to my apartment. I began losing more feeling and was forced to call for an ambulance because I was lightheaded and seeing bright flashes as though from a professional photography session. The ambulance showed up. One of the EMTs was someone I had gone to grade school with. He was red-headed, freckled, Scott, the one who wouldn't kiss me in a game of "Truth or Dare" because he wasn't interested. I was overweight and awkward back in sixth grade. Here he was possibly saving my life. He kept telling me funny stories about our times growing up in Charlestown. When we got to the ER, the doctors thought I was having a full-blown stroke. My family doctor had failed to check my most recent blood work and my blood had gotten too thick without my knowledge. The ER doctor responsible for caring for me gave me a Heparin IV and Demerol without checking my orange allergy wristband with "Allergy to Demerol" printed on it. A nurse angrily snapped at him, "What are you trying to do, *kill her?*" It wasn't looking good for me that day. He told her to stop talking and hand him some medication. She reluctantly followed his orders. The nurse's prediction almost came true in the following few minutes. My heart rate dropped below sinus. It slowed down so much that I had a sucking, churning sensation in my chest, a sudden heaviness, and vision so blurry that I could barely see anything. Luckily, I could hear everything.

I was too angry to die; therefore dying was out of the question. The nurse was giving the doctor the "I told you so" speech and he apologized to me in my altered state. With a trembling voice and tears in his eyes, he barked, " Grab (a certain dose) of epinephrine now so she doesn't crash!" I told him with all of my remaining strength, "I told you I was allergic to Demerol." He just kept apologizing, staring at the heart monitor, and squeezing my wrist for my pulse. Once again, I was too close to death for comfort, deciding that from now on I would take control of my health using both traditional and non-traditional medicine to keep my body operating properly.

My then doctor, Dr. O'Dell, came into my trauma room. I decided to absolutely give him a piece of my mind and relieve him of his shoddy service toward me. I told the nurse very sternly, "Get that witch doctor out of here." Then he still proceeded to come into the room. That was it! I let him have it. I said, "You didn't have time to read my lab results and here we go again. I'm not going to give you another chance to almost kill me. Get out of here. You are relieved of your responsibility to me. Just stay away from me, Dr. O'Dell." With that farewell, he was gone. He was replaced by a female Ivy League, albeit rather snooty, doctor. She was thorough, but a bit judgmental, and not able to relate very well to someone my age. For example, one time I was wearing a short stylish skirt and she began a lecture about safe sex! I was deeply offended. She was the original anti-feminist. I told her that I had virtues of steel and that my sex life, or absence thereof, was nobody's business. She said she treated every patient the same way as symptoms can indicate a variety of illnesses. This was her reasoning for running unnecessary tests which I suppose was better than not enough tests. She was annoyingly prejudicial but I liked that she was the polar opposite of Doctor "I Don't Know How to Analyze A Blood Test" O'Dell. I kept the same neurologist because he was an excellent medical detective. He had been wonderful at piecing together and explaining the parts of a transient ischemic attack (TIA), or stroke, together in a way that was helpful and decisive. This mild stroke was a major life-changer. I was put on medicine that I will have to take for the rest of my life pending a medical breakthrough during my lifetime. At first, this fact was literally a bitter pill to swallow. The bottom line was for me to do everything I could to stay in the land of the living. The neurologist told me that I was experiencing some short term memory loss and that I had to take each day one at a time. He advised me to often look at a calendar and carefully keep track of the date and time. He also told me to try not getting frustrated if I was unable think of a person's name or recall something that I should know normally. My doctor also told me to drop the semester since I had lost two weeks during my long hospitalization at South County Hospital, the same one

I had candy-striped at in High School. I had to get back to work. The group home agency didn't want me back, claiming that my fill-in was working out well and that they didn't think that hands-on work was something that I needed at that time. I took the first job that I could handle, as a customer service booth worker at the local grocery store for several dollars less per hour that the group home had paid me. The store also couldn't give me full-time hours because they felt I would soon leave to return to college full-time. I was a part-time minimum wage employee with no health benefits. It just about killed my spirit to drop out of college for the semester, a major setback as I was about to declare a double major in both social work and political science. Friends and family visited me at my apartment.

My mother knocked on my door around noon one day not too long after I had gotten my new job. I said, "Mom, you never told me we were getting together today." She replied, "I just told you again over the phone last night to remind you. Don't you remember?" The tears came immediately. Weeks' worth of frustration with my slow-to-repair-itself memory came pouring out. I sobbed, "Mom, it's been a few weeks now and I can't remember anything, not even what day it is. I feel so stupid Mom and I wonder if I'll ever be the same again. Am I always going to be this lame-brained? Because I hate it!" Mom handed me a coffee and sandwich saying, "You've just had a mild stroke, if you forget an occasional day or appointment, then consider yourself lucky. You need to start looking at your calendar and get your newspaper delivered daily to keep track of what day it is. Just be happy that you are alive, Lara, because you had another close call."

Mom is often correct as she was in my "mild stroke" aftermath. Although I was greatly distressed over my apparent memory loss, there were ways to get my brain rewired correctly. My decision was to take my mother's advice and retrain my mind to its former functioning. Medical bills began showing up that were not being covered by my college plan since I had to drop out for the semester.

I got a sinking feeling in my stomach as I wondered how I would pay for my medical bills, rent, and utilities. Forget food. Food was last on my list. The previous semester, I had done a research project on a local homeless shelter. Knowing how easy it was to become homeless, I decided to do anything short of working myself to death to never let that happen. What does anyone do when she has very little income, mounting medical bills, and is afraid of starving because she won't take charity? She writes a letter to Oprah Winfrey asking if she can help. I wrote a letter to one of my idols and one of the strongest women on the planet in hopes that she would know somebody who could help me in this seemingly hopeless situation that I found myself in. I received a reply a few weeks later that read something like, "We are sorry. Your situation, although serious, is something we cannot assist you with at this time." Not even Oprah could help.

I dropped out of college, got full-time hours at the grocery store with no benefits, and found out that the income was not enough to pay for my medical prescriptions and lab work. The day that this reality hit home was a truly depressing one. I was raised by parents who taught me to just work harder through the tough times to stay afloat and to never take charity. That last part of their teaching about never taking charity rattled my mind over and over again like a jackhammer. What was I going to do? There was no special program for college men and women who suddenly come down with a freak illness that most of America had not heard of. The first step that I took to get help was to go to the Catholic Church. As a lifelong Catholic, I had often donated time and food to local food banks and church-affiliated organizations. I did this throughout my upbringing and in college as part of a sorority and the college Christian Youth Group. My hope was not to take one red penny from the state, so any humiliation suffered at the Catholic food bank was worthwhile. Besides, my roommate, John, was worried about the bare fridge on my side of it, constantly asking me if I was eating enough. The woman at the food bank front desk was very rude, looking through me instead of at me. I guess I was a very stylish broke and hungry woman who didn't quite look the part. She punitively demanded my life story which I reluctantly gave. I begged her to never tell the local newspapers because it could hurt my family's political life in my old hometown if it ever got out that I'd been to the local bread bank.

She promised confidentiality which made me breathe a sigh of relief. When she heard my reason for coming in, she looked sad. She directed me to her supervisor who said that until my medical bills were paid off, I could use the food bank, exclaiming to me, "You poor thing. You are so young to be given such a large cross to bear. God bless you and take care of yourself during this difficult time." Then she grabbed me by the hand and showed me where all of the food was. I took one loaf of bread, ashamed of the whole affair. She stopped me and said, "Do you need bagels? Here are some bagels. Take as much bread as will fit in your freezer. Do you need milk? What kind do you drink?" I nodded to the 1 % milk, because if I spoke a word, I would break down crying, which isn't good when you are trying to be a tough, starving twenty-four-year-old. She kept on asking, "Do you need anything else to drink? Would you like some dessert? How long has it been since you had some fresh cookies?" I answered all of her questions with a shaky voice, trying to keep my composure the best that I could.

The formerly-defensive woman was now making sure that I had enough food to make it through the week. God bless that woman, wherever she is. I never went to bed hungry after that day. That was the day that I learned that taking charity is sometimes necessary to survive. I thanked God for my big secret, the local food bank. One of my friends who knew me very well, a professor from my college, Ronald Kozack, a white-haired, short-statured, happy family man, was also my medical power of attorney since my near-death experience the year before. He used to go through my checkout line at the grocery store at the old A & P . He taught Business Mathematics. We used to talk about school and life, developing a friendship that transcended age and walks of life. My balding, married, middle-aged friend was surprisingly at my apartment door with a bag or two of food that he too had gotten from a local food closet. His wife made me a delicious homemade pie.

After crying and hugging him for a minute or two, I cried, "So you are psychic as well as being a wonderful friend?" He said, "We've all had times like this in our lives. You've just had too many of them. God's testing you right now. You aren't helpless, Lara. You are a hardworking young woman who is going through a hard time. Do not feel badly for having to rely on friends right now. We are all pulling for you at the university. As a matter of fact, your instructors and I have a little something for you. Do not open this until I am gone. Let's just say that when I bumped into your friends and professors on campus, they said that they can't wait to see you back in class again. Also, here is the state medical assistance number. I know you can't afford health insurance currently, so call this number immediately for help over the next few months. Yours and my tax dollars paid for it, so don't feel bad using it. It is the only way that you can see the doctors that you need to see and have necessary testing done. Now is not the time for pride, but for healing. You will be back in college next semester. I am going to help you to get back to school and get back to the old Lara again, period."

We took the bags of food into the kitchen. I kept thanking Ron. He hugged me, handed me a sealed business envelope, and quickly left. Later that evening, I opened the envelope to find a letter signed by many of my professors and fellow students wishing me well, as well as a check in the amount of four months' rent. It looked like I would be receiving proper medical attention and would keep a roof over my head thanks to a whole lot of love from the folks at the University of Rhode Island.

Ron was a beyond-the-call-of-duty friend, a person who always gave from the heart and never expected a thing in return. He was a truly wonderful human being. I miss him every day. I got to see several specialists that Ron knew to be the best of the best in Rhode Island, every physician specialist type we could think of. I found out what had caused the clotting and was relieved to know that with careful monitoring it could be prevented for the rest of my life. It is such a weight off of you when you finally go to a medical specialist who looks at you as a person, not merely an object. I felt human again, truly alive. I was back in control of my body again. A neuropsychiatrist tested my memory, IQ, behavioral condition, and performed other mental evaluations. I tested above average on all levels which made me very happy. The neuropsychiatrist said, "I did not test you before the stroke, but you have zero cognitive deficits, testing above average on all fronts. You are fortunate to have no detectable brain deficiency." I could have skipped out of the hospital after the doctor came back with those promising test results.

Ron accompanied me to all of the physician specialist appointments that I made. He said, "We live in a world with a very chauvinistic, male-dominated, medical community. I'm here to make sure that they really listen to you without giving you the 'just a hysterical female' brush off." I have tested this theory and unfortunately with some doctors it is very true, although it is not common to receive this treatment. If any woman would like a kinder, less chauvinistically-biased examination by a male doctor, she should bring along a male friend. The doctor's change in attitude will get the woman fumed, but at least she will get the treatment she deserves and needs. It is better than having her gender used against her to her possible medical detriment.    As I began to feel more and more energetic over time, I began seeking alternative therapies. I began to see a Chinese herbalist and acupuncturist at a place called The Center of Balance in East Greenwich, Rhode Island. I wanted treatment that had stood the test of time for many thousands of years to compliment traditional medicine. My acupuncturist was excellent. My circulation noticeably improved over a matter of weeks. She used hot stones and burning incense to heat the needles, focusing on the parts of the body that control pain and circulation. It was amazing. Her business name was very appropriate as she was definitely helping me to regain my physical balance for which I was very thankful.

Alternative medicine was just catching on in mid-1990s New England. I suppose it took time to travel from the western to the eastern United States. The treatment I received increased my circulation and restored my energy levels back to normal. You cannot put a price on feeling well-put-together and they were not inexpensive at forty-five dollars per session once per week. Health insurance did not cover treatments there, but she was a compassionate person, charging me a lower college student rate.

I enrolled in college for the next semester. Since I still used a cane to help me keep my balance on uneven ground, I had to use campus handicapped tags to travel from class to class. I still fell a few times in the ice, snow, and slush but I was never late for class. My professors helped to get note takers for all of my classes since I had extreme weakness and numbness remaining on my right side from the stroke. My hand would give out after only a few sentences. There were still glitches that I had to work out mentally as far as recall was concerned. For example, I had many men and women call me by name that I could not identify on sight. I had no idea who they were. One woman asked, "You don't know who I am, do you?" I told her sorry, that I didn't. She said cheerfully, "Don't worry. I heard about what happened and you'll get your strength back. See you later, Lara." To this day, I still do not know who many of the folks were who said hello to me immediately after the stroke unless it was a person who I had a lot of contact with on a regular basis before my sudden illness.

It was so frustrating to have forgotten recent events and names in my life in the months following my stroke. Some of my memory never came back. It is like that saying, "If it was really important, you would not have forgotten it." It didn't matter. I would create more memories to fill the gaps that those moments of limited oxygen left in my mind. My memory wasn't the only aspect of my mind to be affected by the stroke. Several months afterward, I had just lain down to fall asleep when the unthinkable happened. Seconds after turning off the television, I heard the loudest androgynous scream in my right ear. I jumped out of my bed in fear. *Was this a ghost? Was my imagination playing tricks on me? Or even worse, was I losing my mind?* It was after midnight, but I immediately called my mother, a registered nurse who could offer a much-needed voice of reason.

After telling her what had just happened she said, "This happens with stroke patients quite frequently and temporarily. If it happens only once, then I would say you are lucky. Call me back if it happens again and we will call the neurologist, otherwise chalk it up to being oxygen-deprived and sleep-deprived from your stroke. Your brain is rewiring, so you may have sensory and emotional symptoms for a while. It is all normal. You are not crazy. Now, get to bed. The thing you need to do most right now is to rest." I thanked my Mom. Thank God I wasn't crazy, although I sure felt like it some days. I do not ever want to hallucinate again. It was the scariest experience ever. My dating life was officially suspended until I felt normal again. The last thing I needed was a "sympathy" date. That's when someone knows you have some affliction and figures that you will forget their extremely obvious permanent flaws in lieu of your own impending normalcy. It does not work and never will. All I could do was focus on my health, then work, and last but not least beginning my junior year spring semester of college. Oh, yes, and paying for a two-week hospital stay for the rest of my natural life, all seventy-five thousand dollars of it. Our health care system is so badly flawed that a person can go bankrupt a few months after hospital discharge for inability to pay the bill. I have seen adults of all ages go through this financial strain working in the mental health field. It can be devastating for a family, even worse than the illness that got the family the bills in the first place.

When my professor friend Ron told me how much I owed the hospital, I was sure that I would have to drop out of college to pick up a second, or third, job. Ron said that he knew the chairman of the hospital board of directors and said he would find out how I could repay my debt over time. I thanked him for doing so. The next thing that happened was unexpected and unimaginable. Ron had gone to my professors as well as to the financial aid office to tell about my sudden illness. They all pitched in whatever they could, Ron presented it to the hospital chairman, and my bill was paid through a special program created for special cases like mine in which the patient had no choice but to be hospitalized for an extended period of time.

I was so thankful. The generosity shown toward me by both friends and total strangers was overwhelming to say the least. My self-esteem hit a new low as I felt even more like a charity case, but returning to campus improved my outlook on life considerably. Former classmates who I couldn't remember came up to give me hugs and to tell me how happy they were to see me walking, talking, and back on campus. One of my fellow social work majors, a gorgeous African American woman with a large build and huge smile always gave me a thumbs-up anywhere that we ran into each other on campus. It made me feel so much better to know that people in my academic life were pulling for my recovery.

My sudden illness had caused me to be isolated from my former life. A new Lara was returning where the old Lara had once stood. My former physical well-being was slowly on its way back. My three favorite very feminist, strong, and honest Human Development and Family Studies faculty members used my story to teach fellow students about the social, emotional, and economic impacts of a sudden illness on an individual and their family members. At first, I was an unwilling poster child. Once I had gotten over myself, I realized that the other students could use this knowledge to help others like me who suddenly became seriously ill or almost died from an illness. In this case, I was happy to tell my story as a warning against prolonged use of birth control pills and to help my classmates to help others who had similar medical situations.

At times I became overwhelmed with the thoughts of those scary incidences and would have to stop to take deep breaths to continue talking about it. The birth control pill may have changed my blood chemistry, something that was not clearly explained on the warning label.

More women have strokes from using birth control pills than many would like to think. An expert in the field of stroke and blood clots that cause stroke from the Netherlands did an extensive study of female stroke victims both users and non-users of birth control pills, in 2002. This scientist discovered that the risk for stroke doubles for women on the birth control pill. The exact number was 6 in 10,000 pill users. Only three non-users had strokes. The risk for blood clots and strokes in women who take the pill is 2.4 times greater than a non-user, to be exact, according to the leading expert in birth control side effects, Ale Algra. You can look at his study results at www.cbc.ca/news/story/2002/02/07/pill020207.html. I have yet to see that specific a warning on birth control pill pharmaceutical literature, but hope that changes as soon as possible. The warnings must include more accurate statistics on the actual pill information label to prevent more unnecessary sudden illnesses or deaths in women who use them. The pill is not the only excellent means of birth control available to women. Birth control pills are a great invention, but women should be told honestly about all of the medical risks of taking them, period. One of my favorite professors in the Human Development and Family Studies department had Lupus. She, although now deceased, was a wonderful woman formerly from Maine with a Maine woods cutting dry sense of humor that I really had to use my mind to truly appreciate. She and I became very close due to our "bad blood" as she would refer to it. We understood each other's poor circulation, getting sicker than most (due to lowered immunity) , including those we caught the viruses from. When people have an immune deficiency they usually get whatever contagious illness that is going around. With almost all blood-related illnesses, sufferers get a lowered immunity and sometimes a lowered white blood cell count. As though these factors are not alarming enough, they also get very sick from common ailments when most people get nothing more than a sniffle or low-grade fever.

Oddly, yet appropriately enough, my professor's nickname was "Bloody" due to an uncommon last name and her illness. Dr. "Bloody" explained, "God, or the Goddess if you prefer, gave us bad blood. We'll just have to have bad blood together. Whenever you don't feel well, I'm here for you. I know how depressing it can be when your body doesn't do what you want it to do."

It seemed as though I had met every vampire in the state for the endless blood work that followed my stroke. I call them vampires because until modern medicine streamlined the finger prick method, blood was sucked out the old-fashioned painful way with a select-a-size needle. I actually have scar tissue from all of the times that I have been stuck by needles in my arms. Instead of only focusing on my less-than-ideal health, I returned to classes full-time to quench my insatiable thirst for knowledge. You can never learn too much about this world we live in or the people in it, at least that is my personal mission statement.

For a science requirement that I had to complete for my major general education requirements, I chose Volcanology. Volcanoes 101 was taught by one of the world's leading volcanoligists: an Icelandic professor named Dr. Siggurdsen. His class was extremely difficult, but equally fascinating. The math and chemistry were so over my head that I had to pay for a tutor on a sliding scale to get extra help from the class's teaching assistant. Without her help, I am sure that my grade would have been abysmal. I achieved such a low score on one of my exams that I broke down only seconds after I saw the grade. I excused myself from the room.

*Why had I cried? I am tougher than that*, I thought. *What is wrong with me? Why are my emotions so close to the surface?* I called everyone I could think of that day, family, friends, and physicians to help me with my sudden tendency toward tears and raw emotion.

All said that this, too, was an aftereffect of the stroke that would pass with time. I experienced three months of embarrassment due to self-control issues. Luckily, I made it through the semester with passing grades, even a B- in Volcanology, although some insensitive ignoramus left a box of tissue on my desk before each one of my torture-via-chemistry volcanoes classes. Each time, I would throw it in the garbage and calmly retake my seat. It was my way of saying, "You are not allowed to insult me or consume my precious energy, you compassionless, immature person." Throwing the tissue box away became therapeutic with the added bonus of releasing some anger in a healthy way. I was no longer mired in the sadness that had prevailed since the stroke had struck. A very young, blue-eyed, blond-haired man would hold my books and the door for me since I still walked with a cane. He walked me to my car every day after class that semester without caring what anyone thought. My classmate explained, "Someday, if I get hurt, I want someone to be nice to me, too." I always gave him a hug before getting into my car to leave. He was a surrogate brother that semester whether he realized it or not. God put so many wonderful people in my life after my stroke who supported me while I regained my strength. By semester's end I had an improved perspective on my future and more control over my medical issues. When the warmer weather came, the need for a cane and acupuncture lessened. I gave up the cane completely by the beginning of the summer break. I had to take summer classes to make up for the courses I had missed during the previous school year. I had a lot of catching up to do in order to be more marketable to social service agencies going into my senior year. The commute from my apartment to the college was getting to be more of a hassle as I had begun to work for a new group home agency in Newport, Rhode Island, which was forty-five minutes from my apartment in Westerly. It was time to get a place closer to my job and the university. The opportunity for a better living situation came just as the semester ended. Ron knew a business professor whose in-laws needed a live-in assistant since they were frail and elderly with social service needs. Ron told them who I was. He was an excellent agent who let them know that I was trustworthy and that I had worked in the mental health field for several years. The McNairs hired me just as my lease came up for renewal in May. In exchange for caring for them, providing a sanitary environment, and monitoring the couple's safety, I would live in a private wing of their home rent-free. I would pay for my utilities with the exception of the heating bill which was covered by the family who controlled the thermostat.

I had a small living room, a 10x10 bedroom, and a 7-foot porcelain soaking tub, perfect for those days when I worked two to three jobs, second and third shifts at my various jobs. Two Chinese foreign exchange graduate students, a husband and wife, had lived there before, taking care of Aidan and Alicia Thomas, the very adorable, sweet couple whom I would grow to love over the year and a half that I lived there. My direct supervisors were a Catholic couple with young adult children, a son and daughter, who lived with them. The Thomases daughter, Linda, was the primary caregiver, both a wonderful daughter and great person to work for. Her brother, who lived nearby, visited only on major holidays and was a haughty clinical school psychologist who knew it all. The one thing he did not know was how to connect emotionally with his own parents, which I found to be very sad.

He was a fair-weather child. If there was a crisis, he could not be counted on, so Linda gave up calling on him. He hardly showed his face, but when he did I would make *hors d'oeuvres*, desserts, and other treats for His Highness. He would visit for no more than about an hour, then disappear for another half-year, give or take. I was not a big fan of his. My laboring before his visits was exclusively for the Thomases, never for their arrogant son, his extremely high-maintenance wife, or strangely melancholy, although sweet, little boy. This was a perfect live-in situation for my senior year, a job on campus working for seniors while maintaining my other jobs to pay my bills. Seniors have always held a special place in my heart because they have "been there, done that," with wisdom that we could all learn from if we all listened better.

Aidan, a World War II veteran, had Alzheimer's disease. Alicia, a beautiful former Brit in her late 80s was physically frail but very strong mentally, only with periodic anxiety attacks from worry over her husband's condition. She was also self-isolating by refusing to interact with others her age outside of the home. They respected my privacy and it was mutual. I prayed every night that I would never have roommates again. At age twenty-four, I did not want any more strangers under my roof. My professor friend, Ron, had found me a private wing of a house on campus which not only improved my GPA, but my finances and medical condition, as well. My self-esteem was nearing full strength again.

That summer, I took care of the Thomases, took two summer classes, worked with teen girls in state custody in Newport, and worked as a security guard at local industrial centers such as a computer chip firm and an international soap production plant. Aidan would ask where I was hiding my twin sister. Alicia always asked how I did it. I just told her that I liked paying my bills and having a little money left over for personal expenses. Nothing could stop me from achieving my goal of becoming a professional social worker. In order to remain financially stable, I had to put a lot of money into my bank account for the following school year. Three jobs was a breeze as I looked forward to my senior year and upcoming career opportunities. It didn't matter how hard I had to work, I just did it in hopes of a brighter future. My time on active duty in the U.S. Army after high school, and each of my college jobs, gave me skills that I believed would help me to attain excellent post-college employment.

Working with the five teenagers in Newport was exciting, a welcome change in gears from elder care. The group home had been a funeral home at one time, a stately late 1800s Federal-style estate with four front pillars and a large viewing window on the first floor for the deceased. It was both symbolic of the condition of the American family and at the same time ironically bizarre to have victims of dying or dead American families in a place that the dead had once occupied. The girls were, unfortunately, in various stages of abandonment and recovery. Some of the girls had committed crimes and were just released from the "Kiddy condos" which is what the girls called the Rhode Island juvenile detention center in Cranston, Rhode Island. It was rewarding being a supportive mother-sister figure in their lives. They were the first children that I helped do homework with and prayed with before they went to bed each night if they wanted to. I cared for all of the girls equally, so it really bothered me when they sometimes fought with each other.

Some of the girls had inadequate parenting by drug and alcohol addicts who were undergoing rehab or refused to get help. Some had come from very functional families and had succumbed to mental illness or indulged in dangerous criminal activity usually reserved for those who are born into poverty, only they were from upper- and middle-class backgrounds. As one of their caseworkers, I counseled them, dispensed psychotropics and other medications, and mediated at times between the girls and their family members who visited during Sunday afternoon visiting hours. It was a lockdown facility with security cameras in various areas of the beautiful old Federal-style estate that was purchased by the state of Rhode Island for its Department of Children, Youth, and Families for child placement purposes. My job there was to try to give the girls a sense of safety and to help them to function in society again, with or without the support of their biological families. My supervisor used to get angry with me for giving the girls too much "freedom" and would say that "freedom could get girls like these into a lot of trouble very quickly." In other words, he wanted to keep the girls locked up and out of step with other children their age. All the same, I took the girls out to age-appropriate safe activities often, such as roller skating, ice skating, and hanging out at the mall with the help of at least one other staff member.

The girls loved their weekend excursions, listening to CDs on my stereo or in the van, having fun with other young people, especially young men in their age group. Exchanging phone numbers and hand-holding were their limits for co-ed interaction. I thought these limits would help the girls to stay out of mischief, yet would give them some release from their isolation at the group home. My supervisor nagged me about giving the girls too much independence and blah blah, but I would pacify him by repenting for my wicked free-thinking ways to remain working with my wonderful adolescent girls who had somehow fallen through the cracks of our society. These young women deserved to feel empowered, intelligent, and part of a functioning family. We were all part of a big temporary family at the group home. My work with "the girls" as I affectionately called them led me to an internship working with at-risk youth in the dangerous gang-rich area of Central Falls in South Providence, Rhode Island, the fall semester of my senior year. I stayed at the group home in Newport, remained working for the McNairs, and quit my security officer job due to very low pay and terrible graveyard shifts. Working graveyard shift was sapping my energy for college coursework, as well as my social life. Also, I can't stand working third shift because I always gain weight. In order for me to stay awake in the guard enclosures, I would use sugary sweets and too much caffeine to stay alert. I listened to episodes of *Seinfeld* on my radio those long nights in the "guard shack." Those *Seinfeld* episodes are so funny and so well-written that even without a television screen Jerry, Elaine, George and the crew kept me laughing and my mind sharp as I became a zombie version of myself. Also, some of the workers and truckers were perverted. As a somewhat attractive woman in my mid-twenties, the men thought they should constantly ask me out, had permission to constantly flirt, and that because of my tough job any sexually suggestive comment would roll off my back. What they didn't know was that I was a female Army veteran armed with a night stick and pepper spray. Having to put up with that nonsense for five years in the military was bad enough, but to voluntarily put up with similar treatment in the civilian sector was just plain foolish.

My peace of mind and sufficient sleep were far more important than proving to the rest of the world that I should be taken as seriously and treated with the same respect as my male security guard co-workers. There were better ways to prove my strength as a woman and this situation was not it. We didn't even get as high an hourly wage as our male counterparts with gender being the only difference in deciding our different hourly pay rates. Seniority did not mean much in that particular outfit. Other women who pulled security felt the same way that I did, but like me they, too, needed money for college and had a steady flow of bills to pay, so there they were. Women should demand respect in the workplace without facing the threat of being mistreated or fired. Women should also be making one hundred percent of the dollar a man makes. It will take a majority of women in this country to help change the laws and get equal pay in the American workplace.

*Chapter Eleven*

My last oil change was a long time ago and my engine is running dirty.

It was the beginning of my senior year for my undergraduate degree. I was thrilled, although preoccupied with the sensible fear of the unknown regarding my near future in the full-time adult workforce. *Where would I live? Where would I work?* These questions still arise in adulthood from time to time for the majority of Americans. Fear of personal life change can be terrifying. I knew this constant self-examination consuming my thoughts was grueling, essential, and, thankfully, temporary. The answers to these life-altering questions were no less difficult to find answers for. The Alternative Learning Placement (ALP) center in Central Falls was a tough and, at the same time, very rewarding internship venture. The director was an extremely friendly, lovely, robust, balding gay gentleman named Roger who immediately took a friendly mentor tone toward me and my fellow interns giving us nicknames a few days into the internship. The nickname that Roger gave me was "Buffy" from *Buffy the Vampire Slayer*, a strange program geared toward teens at that time. It starred a brunette actress who bleached her hair light blond, as I did at the time.

Roger set the ground rules as to what I and the other interns could discuss with the children. The children were mostly teens aged thirteen-to-fifteen who had been in trouble with the law or had trouble at home that affected their schooling. He told us that we were about to be fed to the sharks, however the "sharks" were still children who needed an excellent public education and compassion. He told us that compassion was something they had not gotten much of in life. These kids were some of the toughest to work with because they were being forced by their parents, the school system, the judicial system, or some combination of the three into being sent to the ALP.

Roger assigned me to teaching life skills with the task of finding local speakers to come in to tell the kids how they had succeeded against the same odds that these teens were now facing. My students were amazing, but it took a monumental effort on my part to build trust with them. They were already experts at having adults let them down.

It was my first day solo with the ALP students. As soon as the children entered the classroom, a Caucasian, loud-voiced young lady said, "Who the Hell sent in rich girl over here to teach us? What the f--- is she gonna teach us, etiquette or some sh--?" Then an African American young man said, "Just what we need, a lily-white-assed teacher-in-training who wants to save some little ghetto kids like us. Man this is some bullsh--! What does some white girl know about saving my ass? SSShiiiiii_," he said with a giant sigh. I decided that my Laura Ingalls prim and proper dress shirt and skirt ensemble wouldn't work with these children. I was determined to get a wardrobe change to let them focus attention to the message, instead of the appearance of the messenger.

After cutting me down to about the size of an ant, the teens allowed me to speak about the reason for us meeting together three times per week that semester. I walked around the room with a roster asking the young men and women to stand up, answer, "Here," and state their names. Then, I asked that they write their names, ages, interests, academic goals, future goals or dreams, and one personal issue that they each would like to work through on an index card for me to keep in my teacher's file. Each card also had their name, address, a contact name, and phone number if I needed it for an emergency or any other student issue. I told them who I was, my background, and why I was there at their school. I also told the young woman from the first outburst that at no time would I be teaching etiquette as part of my life skills sessions, but that if she would like to research and present on that particular topic it was permissible. She seemed pleased with my response as a huge smile stretched across her battle-worn face. She told me that she would think about it.

I could hear mumblings and grumblings such as, "She's wasting her time," and "She'll quit today," as they headed out of the building. Mine was their last class of the day. Not one of the children said, "See you Wednesday" or anything else kind as they watched me get into my college compact economy hatchback. With my stubborn Irish and Italian heritage, it just wasn't in me to give up. These kids were our country's future, needing a great education and acceptance to become productive members of society no matter what environmental obstacles got in their way.

Senior year was proving to be a stable foundation-building experiment with the near future of having a social work degree and being able to help others with the knowledge I had gained. Aidan and Alicia's needs did not interrupt my senior year schedule. I planned my activities around housekeeping, Aidan's adult day-care drop off, Alicia's senior center visits, hair salon appointments, and their grocery store excursions. Their daughter Linda was always very pleasant, letting me know about the Thomases' appointments, et cetera. The Thomases' son was slightly annoying. Living only forty-five minutes away, he showed his face for about an hour on holidays and an occasional birthday. Otherwise, Mr. School Psychologist did not seem to want to be around the two people who created the lungs that breathed the same air that theirs did. It was most likely because the two had separate emotional issues. They just were not perfect enough for him. Personally, I like people who practice what they preach. If you are supposed to be a therapist, then be a compassionate empathetic individual instead of a narcissist.

As one of my psychology professors once said, "Anyone who believes he or she is perfect is absolutely insane." John, the extremely distant son, was no treat. He would complain about the forty-five minute drive and the responsibility of raising his only child, his son, and what a struggle it was. How hard can it be raising one child unlike the rest of the country's families that contain at least two children on much smaller salaries than his? I would hide in the other room wanting to regurgitate. The really sad part is that Aidan and Alicia ached to see him and praised him to Jesus himself after he, his insecure meticulously well-maintained wife, and unusually-quiet son would leave. John most likely loathed having parents with emotional issues stemming from his father's Alzheimer's diagnosis because he didn't show up often. I had to bite my tongue often in his presence as even his punch lines were highly insensitive to all present. John the Magnificent was no saint and I wondered how a person like him could be any good for a young school student who had real problems. Talking to John almost put me in an altered mental state, so imagine his effect on the youth of Somerset, Rhode Island.

The Thomases' son-in-law, Linda's husband Talbot, was no walk in the park. He would insult them in front of Linda and me. His jokes were never funny. I could see the anguish on Linda's face that her husband could be so cruel. Linda had three older children to oversee, plus her parents to care for. They rented the house we lived in for Aidan and Alicia. Linda also worked in a medical research lab. It was no glamour job, but she never complained because it gave her some financial independence from her controlling accountant husband. She had heaps of responsibility and unlike her pompous brother, never complained about it. With fibromyalgia, Linda went for massage therapy at least once per week. She always took her parents to their doctor's appointments. It pleased me to help take away some of Linda's seemingly overwhelming responsibility that allowed her to focus on her own and her immediate family's needs. Linda was a sweet person. Aidan and Alicia were fortunate to have her devotion whether they realized it or not.

My internship at the ALP was getting better when the number of insults diminished. The kids collectively decided that I was alright for a "white girl" on a mission. Their stories were all different; their only shared similarities were music, accessories, and street addresses. One girl had an absentee father and her mother was, as she referred to her mother's career choice, an "exotic dancer". The other children would snicker, but I would tell them not to make fun of anyone's mother or father in my class. The girl continued to explain how she, too, wanted to be an exotic dancer because it looked exciting and guys "bought you nice things." I told her that if she stuck with school and did well in school, that she could dance as much as she wants, keep her clothes on, and buy herself nice things. She said, "That's doing things the hard way. I'll pass."

One boy of Latino origin told me that his dad was a high school footballer but that he began selling and using cocaine which led to his current prison stint. He said he hated drugs because of where it got his dad. He planned to be a football star like his father, except he would go all the way to the NFL to make his parents proud ,adding that drugs are "no good." He really could not stand drugs. The mention of illegal drugs by other classmates provoked him to verbally bash the offender who brought the subject up. He was my student anti-drug advocate.

Another student, an African American young man, would constantly ask me to show the miniseries *Roots* in class. He was obsessed by "what the man used to do to black folks" and how his ancestors became free men and women. He would explain in graphic detail about what he would do to those "sick slave owners." I told him that the pre-Civil War era was a grim time in U.S. history that must never be repeated. I also reminded him that many Caucasian men and women helped free the slaves through legislation and the

Underground Railroad. I emphasized that not all white people of that era were "sick slave owners."

Career exploration was fun to do with the children. Speakers came in from the community. I scheduled visits by college admissions representatives, community leaders, job corps representatives, police officers, business owners, college athletes, and male and female Army recruiters that I knew through the university. The children figured out that I really wanted to help them to hopefully live better by showing them their many options beyond high school. They were not victims of the ghetto, only of their self-pity, self-doubt, and underestimation of their immense capability to exceed their own expectations in life.

By semester's end the children had spoken to various community leaders and learned about organizations that could improve their lives, such as Big Brothers and Sisters of Rhode Island. I had gotten to know them well over those three months. I hope I inspired those young men and women to give high school a chance because there is a big world out there with so many things to see and many opportunities for the children to excel. The children began to wave goodbye to me by mid-semester. A smile and a wave was more than I could ask for and so wonderful.

The tough crowd that I had met at the beginning of my internship had become like my own children by semester's end. The other interns, teaching staff, and the students had created a haunted house fundraiser together, done mural artwork, and had painted a summer cabin at a wilderness camp for inner city youth in southern Massachusetts. The kids at the Central Falls ALP taught me as much as I intended to teach them. I hope they kept their optimistic hope for the future and carried their high expectations for themselves into adulthood. They were beautiful children. They were all precious young teens who were part of my inspiration to go into elementary education.

Trouble was brewing at the state-affiliated group home for displaced young women. My supervisor was upset about a fender-bending hit-and-run we had gotten in Providence when we took the girls ice skating one cold winter weekend night. The offender rear-ended me and left the scene before any of us could get a good vehicle description or license plate number. My supervisor was also upset because I mentioned seeing rats in the house to residents and staff, unintentionally making a lot of them fearful.

One night I was seated at the second floor office desk writing in the girls' daily behavior journals. I heard a rustling sound behind the adjacent wall to the desk. I chalked the noise up to old, Victorian-era plumbing. Then, I saw plaster fall from the wall from a moving lump behind it. *What in the world was that?* I wondered in a state of high alertness. I figured the girls were having fun trying to scare me in the middle of the night. Then, all of a sudden, a furry brown grapefruit-sized head with beady black watery eyes broke through the plaster wall diagonally from where I sat. It was so frightening that I froze as I wrote my notes down just to lock eyes with it. I screeched with fright into my hand so as not to wake the girls, and ran to the far side of the room, inching my way to the office door without taking my eyes off the freakishly-large sewer rat. I proceeded to hop up and exit the room as quickly as humanly possible.

My coworker ran up the stairs to the office to see what had happened, just catching the rat's head sinking back into the wall, disappearing from view. When I told Kevin about the rat he explained matter-of-factly, "We have never seen a rat in the walls. This home is inspected annually by the state. Besides, there isn't any money in the budget." I responded back to him with my concern for the girls being bitten or that the rats may carry disease. The only thing more disgusting than the disgusting rat that I had seen was Kevin's disregard of the apparent infestation. The girls were not his daughters, nieces, or sisters, so why should he worry about a random sewer rat?

Kevin refused to call a rodent exterminator. I made it my business to constantly remind him that rats are health hazards and can bite the children. He was infuriated with me for implying that he did not care enough about the girls or staff to call an exterminator for the obvious sewer rat problem.

He was also upset because he accused me of being too close to the girls emotionally, that I was not enough of an authority figure for them. I figured they had dealt with nothing but authority figures day-to-day, therefore I preferred taking a nurturer role with them. He was a very cold-hearted man, vicious in fact, who let me know that for "these serious infractions [my] job was hanging by a thread." It was time to find another job.

I decided to take a job completely unrelated to mental health at the local whole foods organic co-op at Lower College Road which now doesn't exist. The owners at the time were a wonderful bohemian couple from New Hampshire. The food and clientele were down-to-earth, plus I got a discount on the healthiest food one can eat. I had never eaten so healthily in my life. I got to take home two-day-old bagels and bakery samples. A co-worker showed me how to cut off the rotten parts of produce to uncover a perfectly edible fruit or vegetable.

The organic coffees were delectable. Starbucks wasn't a Rhode Island establishment at the time in Kingston, yet this organic coffee was better than any chain coffee seller, in my opinion. My favorite was the Sumatra blend. It was the strongest, smoothest coffee that really woke me up on those damp, cold, gloomy New England days. The only product I could not bring myself to use was the environmentally correct, long lasting, one hundred percent cotton reusable maxi pad. That concept was too *Little House on the Prairie* for me. I couldn't imagine taking those things to the laundromat to wash. The alternative medicines, organic foods and beverages sold there were good for me and my health.

I would bring Aidan and Alicia organic food and herbal remedies such as mullein ear oil, a cure for ear infection or water in the ear. Everyone I have recommended it to has told me that if they used the ear drops as soon as they sensed fluid in their ear or ears the oil prevented infection. This remedy worked and prevented the need to spend money and time at a traditional doctor's office. However, some ear infections are too serious and require medical attention. If yours is in this too-far-gone category, seek medical attention immediately. My favorite foods were, and still are, the organic wheat-free pizzas and the Amish cream cheese. If you have never eaten Amish hand-churned cream cheese, you don't know what you are missing. It would come in a huge creamy block which my co-op co-workers and I would cut up, weigh, and sell to customers. I could have eaten the whole thing by myself. It is a melt-in-your-mouth experience. Among other fine things, the Amish make the creamiest, moistest cream cheese that you will ever eat. I live near an Amish market in Maryland, currently, and buy some weekly. My taste buds are still hooked.

The drive to the group home in Newport was beginning to wear on me, especially with the icy, snowy winter weather. Kevin, my supervisor, was no treat to work for. I transferred to a house in North Kingstown, Rhode Island, working for four women, one an aggressive, twenty-something short, burly schizophrenic with psychotic episodes, and another a beautiful, blond-haired, fair-skinned nineteen-year-old paranoid schizophrenic on one side of a duplex. On the other side lived two older women, one was middle-aged with fair skin and red hair who was bipolar with kleptomania. Her roommate was an "out" dark-haired, dark-eyed Native American and African American lesbian who was left with brain damage and severe depression from a horrible car accident several years earlier.

My tough lesbian client had the biggest attitude I had ever encountered. She was trying her hardest to get out of what she called "the system" because she was in a relationship with a woman who was fully functioning. Unfortunately, most state's family and institutional regulations disregard gay men and women as well as their partners, therefore gay men and women are put into scary, unstable situations involuntarily. Most partners at the time had no legal legs to stand on. Her partner was taking legal steps to get her out of the duplex she had been caged in for three long years. Mya was petite and as solid as a power lifter. She had milk chocolate-colored skin and a short afro with an attitude that could be categorized in words as, "I am strong. I am a secure, confident woman. Stay out of my way." Mya, my favorite client at the house, had a huge chip on her shoulder that I felt was justified under the circumstances. She had her two children taken from her because she became so depressed after the car wreck that she tried to kill herself several times unsuccessfully. She showed me the slit scars on her wrists from her suicide attempts. Mya could not wait to lead a normal life with her partner and her children by her side instead of with "the Crazies" as she called her duplex-mates.

Mikala was my second favorite, a nineteen-year-old being forced to live with a three hundred pound psychotic on the other side of the duplex. Mikala was a cheerful, small-framed, thin, pretty, blond-haired, light blue-eyed girl who was too paranoid to leave the duplex, yet wanted nothing more than to be a "normal" teenager. She had straight, shoulder-length hair and a waif's figure. She would often tell me that her medication ruined her appetite. Mikala dreamed of someday taking fashion design courses at the university. We would make many failed attempts to get her to actually step foot on campus to mingle with other people her age. Just as we would get out of my car or the company van, she would screech with fear, begin to cry, and ask to go home.

Mikala also had the linebacker-sized hallucinating violent psychotic roommate to deal with on a daily basis which had to be very nerve-wracking. I did not like working with her and I could not imagine actually having to live with her. One example of Carla's, Mikala's roommate's, psychotic antics was to eat raw meat or animal innards in front of her roommate and staff members in order to try to scare her audience. I remember her doing this with a steak, letting the blood drip down her face onto the linoleum in the kitchen. It is not a pleasant thought for me even today. Once she managed to put fear into someone, she would wait until that person tried to retreat or turn his back and then attack her roommate or staff members. She would attack with every pound of her large-framed, overweight awkward body. She had fists as large as any man's, which made her a true contender when she decided to grab or punch a housemate or staff member.

Her psychiatric record was incomplete, so I wondered how many people and/or animals she had victimized in order to know what to expect. Of course, no such record existed, which failed to help maintain the safety of residents and staff. Group home agencies are notorious for suppressing information regarding client's psychiatric and criminal histories in order to retain staff at a home. Rather than risk losing crucial direct-care staff members, they withhold information which directly affects the safety of residents and staff members. I sensed that Carla could do some damage if she wanted to. She mostly grunted, preferring not to speak. She had already kicked out every window of her side of the house twice, tried to set herself on fire because "it felt good," and had ripped the hair out of a staff member's head, the entire crown area.

Carla's attack on the female staff member was kept secret until my new co-worker came back to work and I witnessed the remnants of the attack. I decided that Carla was dangerous and that I would do my best to avoid her at all costs, even going as far as requesting to work with any of the women except her. She targeted shorter brunette women, apparently because her biological mother was a brunette of short stature who she apparently wanted to hurt. The psychiatrist called her attacks projected violence based on her own fear and hatred of her mother. I didn't buy it for a second. My supervisor promised me that Carla was becoming a new person with the anti-psychotics, anti-depressants, and lithium that they were giving her with her raw gizzards. I was unconvinced of her alleged psychological improvement.

Last but not least was Mary, the short, white-haired kleptomaniac who was severely bipolar with an aversion to human contact after years of sexual abuse at a former state mental facility. She was a kind woman in her forties who loved Disney movies and trying to steal tabloid magazines at the grocery store. Her second favorite items to steal were books about celebrities. Princess Diana had just died and she would grab any magazine with her photo on the cover and say, "I have to have this magazine." Then, when I put the magazine back on the shelf, she would cry to cause a stir among the customers. It was the whole "mean mental health case worker deprives kleptomaniac aging woman of her stolen goods" scenario. Some of you may have witnessed similar scenes.

Mary was the "adult with a two year old affect" whose parent won't cave in to the candy demands, except with an added theft element. Mary never stole anything when she was with me. My supervisor said I was lying because Mary's kleptomania was almost nonexistent when I took her for outings. She would always ask to see a Disney movie. When one came out, I took her to it, popcorn, candy, and the works. Mary was like a happy oversized child emotionally. She smiled throughout the entire movie, even giving me a big hug afterward in the theater lobby. She said that for years she had asked to see a Disney movie, but that my supervisor had told her that it wasn't an "age appropriate" activity. I told her not to worry, that I would smooth things over with her. I suggested to my supervisor that individuals of all ages enjoy watching Disney movies, so why should our clients be any different? She finally spoke the truth when she said, "Because there is lack of funding for unnecessary activities like going to the movies."

The lead woman at the group home claimed that the client's Social Security Disability checks were not enough to pay for paid outings such as to museums or movie theaters. She was one of the most corrupt group home professionals I have ever worked with. I wouldn't be surprised if she pocketed the extra cash herself since as far as we knew she was having the mortgage and utilities paid by the state, using food stamps for groceries, and the women were forced to purchase their clothing at consignment.

I had landed at a group home agency that was corrupt. I was repulsed at the thought of anyone taking advantage of individuals who required assistance with their daily living. They were being stolen from, without complaining at all, either because they lacked the mental awareness to realize it, or had given up trying to fight back. This was not the first time that I had seen group home residents treated as second- or third-class citizens. The adolescent girls at the home in Newport had to deal with their fair share of state money mishandling when I worked there too.

The group home in North Kingstown had its own set of problems, not of the rodent kind, thankfully. At this group home, the supervisors wore designer duds, ate gourmet meals in front of the residents, and the best they could do for the four women who lived there was trips to Wal-Mart, free excursions (not counting fuel costs), and the four walls. These two lead women even rationed the fuel or miles that we case managers could use on our client's excursions, popularly referred to as "outings." It annoys me when ignorant people say that the mentally-challenged somehow have it "better" than most unaffected folks. They had better think again. Yes, a group home is much better than confinement in a mental hospital, however the home's subcontracting agents can sometimes find new ways to cheat the state system. At least that's how it was in two of the three group home agencies that I worked for during my college years. Under their oppressive living conditions, many of my co-workers and I used our own money to take the women out of their home confinement. I could not fathom a life of being stuck in a house day after day with very limited social contact. How are people supposed to reacquaint themselves with society from the sidelines? These women had to re-learn how to play the game of assimilating in a modern, fast-moving American society that our mentally ill or challenged citizens should not be excluded from.

Carla, the psychotic diva, whose jagged black eye liner was sloppily penciled in by staff members and resembled Alice Cooper, was barred from excursions with me because she attacked me the second week of my employment there. I was unlocking the door of her side of the duplex when all of a sudden I was face down on the top step getting punched and kneed violently for no apparent reason. Psychotics never need a reason to attack, so I wasn't expecting one. Luckily, two other co-workers were able to pull her off before the attack got out of control or I got seriously injured. I had scrapes and bruises all over my head, neck, and torso for a week after the violent attack. She later told co-workers that I "took too long opening the door." Carla added that my hair looked like her mother's and that she hated her mother. The female Norman Bates of real life was a client that I refused to work with from that day forward. It was time to look for a post-graduate job out of a group home setting. My plan was to never work in a group home again unless I was running it. Running the home myself would guarantee that the home would be run effectively and ethically.

It was a colder-than-average November. Although I loved a cold New England winter for the beautiful snow and the fantastic skiing up in the northern hills and mountains, it was proving to be bad for my health. My circulation reacted to the cold weather, leaving me with grey and blue fingers and toes if they were unprotected or if I stayed out in the elements for too long. These are symptoms of Reynaud's, a circulatory condition that I had since age twelve, undiagnosed until I was a freshman in college. My elderly couple, Aidan and Alicia needed their driveway shoveled and front steps cleared of ice and snow from a fall snowstorm. Although treacherous at times, I got the job done. The couple used the front door to get the newspaper, to take their dark gray miniature Schnauzer for a walk, and when Linda took the pair to appointments.

As Christmas, one of my favorite times of the year, drew nearer the Thomases wanted white lights strung on the shrubs on either side of the front steps. This seemed like an easy, festive task. As the sun went down, I completed one side of the shrubbery. My feet were ice blocks from the cold. It was time for a break to warm up for a few minutes inside the house. Forgetting the existence of a bottom third step, I stepped out onto nothing. I fell knee and ankle first onto the third icy step. The pain radiating from my inner right ankle was so bad that it took my breath away. The pain was similar to a labor pain or severe back spasm. My knee was pretty skinned up, a bloody blot showed through my sweatpants. My ankle was already swollen. I tried to stand up on my left leg, which I managed well. Then I tried to walk on the right and couldn't, kneeling down in excruciating pain. I got back up, hopping through the snow and ice to the back door where my living quarters were. I called my good professor friend, Ron, to help give me a ride to the emergency room. He rushed over to the house praying, as I was, that it was not broken.

The emergency room doctor, a good looking, kind, reddish-brown-haired green-eyed spectacled young man with a receding hairline asked, "Well, do you want the good news or the bad news first?" Being the eternal optimist I replied, "Please tell me the good news." He told me with a huge smile on his face, "Your ankle bone is fractured only halfway through, so it will not take too long to heal. The bad news is that driving and skiing are out of the question until the cast that I am putting on your lower leg comes off." Hot tears of defeat began to well up in my eyes as I realized that my life would soon undergo some unwelcome changes just as I entered my final year of my undergrad. The doctor continued, "I recommend that you change your injury story to a horrible skiing accident because it sounds so much more intriguing than stringing outdoor holiday lights." I laughed wholeheartedly, while the tears rolled down my face.

One week after my ankle fracture occurred, Linda's husband Talbot paid me a visit. He was the bearer of somewhat-expected bad news as he informed me that I had two weeks to find another place to live. With a casted leg I couldn't drive and could not fulfill my duties to the Thomases. He wanted someone else in there as soon as possible. Ron and I thought his behavior was cruel and a bit odd. Why hadn't Linda broken the news? Why wasn't I given thirty days to find a place to live? Even the worst landlord gave a tenant thirty days to vacate the premises. I told him that I understood. Talbot added, "Don't blame Linda. This was my decision, not hers." Of the latter comment, I was convinced. He continued with a rather chilly tone of voice, "Linda would never kick her parents' elder assistant out onto the street with a cast on her leg and crutches with one semester left of her college degree program," speaking to me as though I was not worth speaking to, as though I was some throwaway object that had lost its usefulness and had to be hastily disposed of. Once again, Ron helped me to find a rental.

I found a house with cheap rent, although it was a house full of hormonal women, three of them, plus an equally hormonal male graduate student. I was the only person tying up my four-year degree and actually looking forward to the real world of work in my chosen field of study. They were on the five-or-more-year degree programs, staying in "college mode" for as long as Mom and Dad were paying the tab. The landlord was a born-again Christian who only rented to college students because she felt she was called to serve Jesus by helping cash-poor people like me to have roofs over our heads during our college years. She had strict rules about parties at the house and was very intrusive regarding our private lives. She had the nerve to look through some of my boxes on move-in day claiming that she was just trying to help me unpack. If you ever wondered why a student who almost has a double major decides to not get the extra twelve credits necessary, look no further than a completely horrific senior year. My living situation was the deal breaker. Not even my love for politics could keep me in this dismal renting situation with some of the most annoying people I had ever met for more than a semester.

The landlady proved to be generally creepy, very left of center, but since I needed the digs desperately, I put up with her nonsense regarding her proclamations such as, "Praise Jesus for your room being available at the exact time that you needed it. It's like when Mary and Joseph were looking for shelter and there it was, like a miracle, in the manger. You were meant to get hurt and come to me." It was quite delusional chat that I had to endure temporarily as I moved through a very inconvenient and all-too-common convalescent spell.

My roommates were all younger, notably immature, and slightly nerdy. They had their own familiar house "lingo," speaking in code so that I would not know what was being said. I had stopped working at the group home but now lived in one. They had the whole "Mommy and Daddy are financing my graduate schooling so I don't ever have to struggle," attitudes. They constantly threw the fact that I had to work in my face whenever they got the itch to do so. "So, how's work? What a shame that you have to work. Your grades probably suffer. I'm so lucky to have parents that value education. I didn't know that social work was so stressful. Why did you get such a low-paying four year?" Need I say more? It was by far the worst and, I am happy to report, the last roommate experience of my life. One of the "nerds" as my close friends referred to them, was a Madonna-worshipping, milktoast, waif-like college cheerleader from Detroit, Michigan. The spastic red-head always had some ridiculous chant bursting from her lips in a lovely Tourette's Syndrome kind of recital. The second female roommate was a psychologist-in-training from Colombia. I don't know what her family did for money, but an Ethan Allen truck showed up one day at the house with a truck load of furniture for the downstairs. She also had constant visits from family who lived in Florida. Her psychologist high horse shtick was really bothering me. I was viewed as the lowly peasant whom she constantly tried to recruit for the personality and neurological tests she had to conduct and study to become licensed. Being a cooperative mental health-advocating peasant, I allowed her to perform the tests, since I was a captive audience with crutches and a "no driving" order for a few months.

My third female roommate was a pretty woman with black hair and brown eyes who was getting a graduate degree in Spanish. She watched NASCAR most of the time with the volume cranked up high. She was tolerable, since she was from the town next to the one I grew up in. She was far from wealthy. She also had a boyfriend that our strange landlady did not know about, or she would have been kicked out of the "born again" college inn. We got along bearably until I got my first true professional position and had to be at work at a certain time. We shared a bathroom, so that did not go over well as she would stay up late and wait until I was finished in the bathroom after which she would complain audibly, saying things like, "Can't you break the other ankle so I can sleep in again without hearing you get ready for work?" and "Miss 'nine-to-five' better get her own place or I am going to go off on her." The niceties were flowing wildly at this rental house.

Last but not least, lest I be called a sexist, was a male Marine Biology major who, like the royalty that he believed he was, had the largest bedroom in the house with its own full bathroom. He was the most difficult to live with because he would have an underage girlfriend overnight every weekend, ate my food, and used my pans to cook his girlfriend up delicious meals. He did this until I told him how disrespectful it was to eat someone else's food without asking to or replacing it. I told him that I was not supporting him nutritionally and to go to the nearest discount store to buy his own pans. I finished by telling him that the "clean them if you use them" rule applied and how I would never have known about the pans had they the decency to clean the cookware after using it. All of my fine roommates knew that, as a temporarily-disabled home-bound college student, I was susceptible to their sophomoric abuse. They uttered every underhanded comment and unleashed whatever nasty dirty tricks imaginable until I healed. After my female friends or family visited, they would utter slurs referring to homosexuality in earshot. After male friends or relatives came over to check on me or run an errand for me, they made rude comments about that, too. If I entered the common areas of the house they would say things such as, "Did she sleep with him? I wonder if she's 'knocked up.'" My family, friends, and I began calling it the Hell House because we were all convinced that these immature individuals were "possessed." They were exceptionally anti-social characters who probably should not have imposed themselves on any other human being. They were all sadistic, each in his or her own "special" way. They did not respect me or my privacy because they were in need of responsibilities and social interaction of their own.

A good friend of mine, Earl, a Narragansett Native American from my hometown ,would do a "police" knock on the front door when he visited. My roommates would jump up and scamper in fear. He scared them with his large build. He was a fitness trainer and weightlifter. He was very tall, dark, handsome, and would give them a look that said, "Don't mess with me." It was wonderful to watch them squirm. For him, it was an opportunity to give a bunch of spoiled adult college students some much-deserved payback for how they were treating me. He said I was a good friend who needed those roommates like I needed a crack in my ankle bone. Ron would pick me up to drive me to campus when he could. We would just sit in his campus office or go out for lunch while we laughed out loud at each other's trials and tribulations. Laughter is always the best medicine, especially when the nonsense flood waters run higher than expected.

I went to the college auditorium to see Maya Angelou ,who gave me such energy to make change with her speech. I knew I had to make life better for myself no matter what action I had to take. Her words, "You have already been paid for. Your ancestors paid for each and every one of you. Now it is time for you to do the same for future generations." She is one of our finest living writers and philosophers. She is inspiration incarnate.

In an attempt to quickly put an end to my senior year roommate horror, I decided to look for a post-graduate social work position. I received two phone calls from positions that I had tried for. The state department of children, youth, and families called to set up an interview, telling me that I did excellently on the state social work exam that I took months earlier in Providence during the pre-crutches era. I was told by a panel of five men and women that I was an excellent candidate. The only drawback was the fact that there were limited positions open for case management. I was told to be patient and find an interim job until I received my job offer in the mail. I had heard of men and women waiting several years for a state social services position.

The second phone call came in from a woman at Bay Community Action Program which was an agency that serviced individuals and families with their human service needs throughout the southern half of the state. The director wanted me to interview as soon as possible because my work experience qualified me for the Case Manager position that was open at Bay CAP.

Ron called to ask me how the job search was going, feeling horribly that there was nothing he could do to improve my living situation since the elder assistant position fell through. I won't tell you what he called his former college of business colleague because it wasn't complimentary. It was rather graphic, actually, and fun to hear from such a mild-mannered person.

I told Ron excitedly, "Both the state of Rhode Island and a state-funded community outreach program contacted me for possible case manager positions!" He prophetically stated, "You'll get one of them. Just be patient." He was very reassuring. It helps you when you have a friend or family member being strong for you when you are feeling vulnerable. Patience, for me, has always been a challenge, but I try very hard to be. I went to my interview at Bay CAP casted for two more weeks and on crutches. It wasn't exactly a grand entrance for an interview recipient. I got several looks of surprise by the director and the three social workers who were already gainfully-employed there at the Narragansett satellite office. All four seemed to be good people, a real change from some of the strange co-workers I encountered at the group homes and previous dead-end college jobs.

Believe it or not, I landed a second interview at Bay CAP. This time, my possible future supervisor asked quizzically, "How soon, exactly, will you be getting this contraption off of your leg?" I answered her, "Not soon enough for me, Pam." Pam laughed softly and then asked how I would like to be an elderly visiting social-work case manager part-time. She added that there was a possibility of becoming a full-time case manager upon finishing my degree program. She told me that my case load number would be in the low thirties, a dream for any starting social worker. Before I left, Pam said, "I once had an office across from your mother and now I will actually have her daughter working for me. It is a small world."

Living in Rhode Island was like being in your own little world. You could be at the farthest end of the state and see at least one person that you knew by name. It is still that way when I visit today. It is a beautiful state with a lot of wonderful people that I will always call "home," no matter where I live. Pam hired me that day and changed my life for the better, whether she realized it or not.

The first thing that I did after beginning my part-time case management job was to save as much money as possible to get my own apartment away from "the Smurfs" as my father not-so-politely called them. Life with the "Smurfs" would come to an end in a few short months. Now the only mumbled insults were "nine to five" comments and gibberish such as "Hi-ho, Hi-ho, it's off to work you go." They could stay in college until they were old enough to draw Social Security as far as I was concerned. Nothing mattered except acing my last semester and excelling at my new social work position.

My senior clients were all so wonderful to get to know and to help. All were in their own unique stages of aging, came from all walks of life, and had individual needs that had to be met. There was a woman who lived in a three-room home without indoor plumbing in a woodsy area of South County. That family was one of the tightest knit families I have encountered in social work. The family was very cooperative, more so than some of the senior's families in their seaside upper-crust sections of the county who somehow found their way to my caseload. The family's main concern was providing their elderly family matriarch with a clean, happy household. She was thrilled to be in a four generation household where she could hold her great-grandchildren. People do not always get that at the nursing facility. A supportive home environment is crucial for physical and mental health for seniors, whether from family members or friends. Loneliness for seniors can literally be a killer. Another interesting client was a blind woman who was a complete self-neglect case. Pam told me that she was on the cusp of being redirected to the state self-abuse case load. She had not yet done herself extreme harm, yet constantly called me to tell me in different ways with each interaction that her health was failing and she would rather be dead.

One gentleman, another living alone, had a nursing assistant-turned-girlfriend in what looked like her mid-thirties, who refused to leave the room when I questioned him. He ended up on the state elder abuse caseload because we discovered that he had given the nursing assistant all of his money. She had used sexual favors to get whatever she wanted from him. Every dollar he had ever earned was gone forever.

On a brighter note, another memorable client, was a former New York Broadway dancer who knew how to "break a leg" and how to get her hands on a bottle of gin. Her openly gay nephew was her legal guardian who had taken her car and driver's license away. She had gotten tired of having no liquor in the house and drove her vehicle through her garage door to get to the town liquor store for, in her words, "some refreshments." I asked her if she had cut the gin and other alcohol out of her daily routine. She said "No, I will leave this world well-preserved thank you." Another question, my least favorite, on the state case management survey was if the client has had regular bowel movements. She exposed her rear end for a millisecond proudly stating, "There is nothing wrong with this ass. I look better than some twenty-year-olds." I just about died from embarrassment. She was in great physical shape, mentally sharp, and "Broadway" brazen. I liked her a lot. It was my best acting job when I kept my poker face on and replied, "Ms. Jones, you seem to be in great health and have a highly competent caregiver in your nephew, so I'll see you in six months, OK?" She told me she would try not to "kick the bucket" until then. I thanked her for that. In the privacy of my car, I enjoyed a therapeutic release in the form of a belly laugh as I left her home for my parents' house for afternoon tea with my mother. The position at West Bay was my favorite case management position thus far because of a manageable caseload, extremely amiable co-workers, and, to this day, the best supervisor of my adult life, Pam. With a stable job in my chosen profession of social work, I was excitedly anticipating college graduation. I was hopeful of becoming a full-time case manager with Bay CAP. My senior clients were a refreshing change from the high-intensity, highly physical group home positions that I had held prior to being hired at Bay CAP. Seniors have their own set of concerns and health issues that many do not take the time to acknowledge. A lot of seniors feel invisible or ignored by mainstream America due to America's obsession with youthfulness. We can all learn a lot from this country's senior citizens. They have been alive longer than we have which makes them experts on the subject of life. If you take time to listen to an elderly man or woman, you will learn some very interesting historical facts. You may learn a few things that you never knew about years past.

It was a reciprocal learning process. My clients learned a few things from me as far as how to adjust to limited mobility and aging bodies, but they taught me a lot, too. My seniors with the best outlooks on life tended to have better health than my clients who focused only on negative aspects of aging. This was a good lesson for my future, to always look on the bright side and possibly live longer in the process. My elderly case manager position was the one steady thing in my life.

My living situation was barely tolerable. The search for my own apartment was soon to be. Goodbye, "Smurfs." Hello, sweet solitude. The one apartment that really caught my eye was in an old turn-of-the-century Colonial, light blue with white trim and shutters. It was a beautiful old building, perhaps a little too close to the railroad tracks, but with a view of East Greenwich Marina out of my living room window. It had an eat-in kitchen with plenty of cabinets for my dishes and decorative touches that I'd collected over the years. There was a lack of separation in the living space for a bedroom, so I would have to create my own privacy with book shelves and an old screen. The landlord was a kind young Italian family-man who said that if I really liked the apartment, he would charge me only $450.00 monthly, which included electricity. That was music to my ears. I told him that I would take it. My neighbors were wonderful. There was a young engaged couple a few years younger than myself upstairs on the second floor. The adult male on the third floor was only there when he was in Rhode Island for business. The neighbor across from me, Kendra, was a cheerful, anything-goes high-spirited person who always had a kind word or two for me when we met up in the hallway or outside the building. She lived with two homosexual male friends, one with spiked platinum blond hair and deep blue eyes, the other with big almond-shaped brown eyes and black hair that was crew cut. Kendra and her roommates were a fun, uplifting group. We became fast friends. They invited me to a drag queen review in Providence which one of the men would be in.

I had never been to a drag show, but my curiosity was piqued and I agreed to attend. Not only were there homosexual men, women, and gorgeous drag queens, but straight-but-not-narrow couples, so I didn't feel like an outcast. The performers were absolutely beautiful, with such glamorous hair, nails, and costumes that were rich-looking, shiny, and full of bling. These ladies were tough acts to follow. A "Madonna" queen came over to tell me how gorgeous my dress was. I told "her" that "she" had better legs than I will ever have. We hugged each other as we enjoyed a good laugh at our own expense. He said he had tricks of the trade to make his legs look thinner than they really were. It was a dazzling illusion.

All of the performances were top notch.

The Cher performer was my favorite. I have been a huge fan of Cher since my 'tween years. Since Cher's daughter Chastity is a lesbian, Cher has become a beloved icon for gay men and women around the world. I admire Cher's gutsiness and shameless interviews. She has the best concert wardrobes and gowns that I have ever seen. The only present popular artist that comes close to Cher's level of creativity is Gwen Stefani, formerly of No Doubt. Gwen Stefani is an excellent artist due to her lyrical courage and her keen sense of all that is hip and outrageously stylish.

My homosexual neighbors at my Greenwich Cove Marina-view-studio apartment building would have a significant impact on my life and forever forge a strong bond between myself and the gay community that I will never abandon. Homophobia is a sickening social disease. We are all God's creations and I believe that we will all be in Heaven together someday, so we had better get along now on Earth. Jesus preached for us to love our neighbors and some of those neighbors happen to be gay.

I admire men and women who are true to themselves, having the courage to "come out" no matter what the rest of society thinks. It was troubling to me when I would see a gay co-worker mistreated based on his or her sexual orientation. Too many states today still have no anti-discrimination laws for gay citizens in their state constitutions. Every state must have anti-discrimination legislation to protect homosexuals in the workplace and the community in the future. It cannot happen soon enough. If you have no gay friends or family members, you have no idea what you are missing. Reach out a hand of friendship to a gay neighbor or relative. You will be happy that you did. They will be happy as well. Mutual acceptance in any human interaction is a beautiful thing that too many take for granted. You can never have too many friends.

My new case manager position was going well. In a few weeks' time, I learned to manage my case notes and home visits to allow me to be ready to go home at 5 p.m., Monday through Friday. One of my co-workers did his notes during lunch time. Another did hers after each visit so that it was fresh in her mind. After lunch, I sat in my car at either a local beach or the Narragansett Pier to listen to the Atlantic Ocean while I wrote my case notes.

My new living situation was an improvement over the odd roommates I had to contend with in the recent past. The only person that I had to answer to was me. The rent was cheap and at least the kitchen was big because I love to cook. I looked forward to having friends over. It was close to my beloved ocean and to a few excellent restaurants that my friends and I enjoyed frequenting. Our favorites were Twenty Water Street on Water Street, and Grille on Main in East Greenwich. Being within walking distance of delicious dining with sophisticated wine lists was an added bonus that I took full advantage of. East Greenwich, Rhode Island, was a small city with a quaint Main Street full of boutiques and eateries popular with both the "It" crowd and some "newly getting by" regular Janes and Joes, like my friends and I were. As you may know, social workers are not usually paid top dollar for what they do, so saving money was crucial to afford occasional luxuries that others with bigger salaries can easily afford.

In order to remain the fashionista and social butterfly that I was known for being, I would save for months to buy key items. I recycled old belts and hats to start my own trend of being eco-friendly as a financial necessity. Luckily, there were some high-end thrift stores, the Salvation Army, and several discount stores close by where I found a lot of fashion and household hidden treasures. After a few months of the same old routine, I became restless for a different place to live outside of little Rhody. After researching jobs online, I found an HIV/AIDS case manager position at a Jewish Family Services organization in Clearwater, Florida. This was a part of Florida near Tampa and St. Petersburg that was known for its excellent white sand beaches and nightlife. The other perk was living in a place that did not often get as cold or overcast as New England often did. Helping men and women diagnosed with HIV/AIDS sounded as rewarding as elder care. The position was salaried with funds provided by the Ryan White Foundation. My mother had relatives down in Sarasota that I could track down if I became too lonely. My mind was made up. In the near future, I would head to Florida to interview for an HIV case manager position.

My spring college graduation ceremony came all too quickly. It was a bright, hot, and sunny May morning with a slight chance of afternoon rain in the forecast. The excitement of actually holding a degree in my hand after all of those years of hard work was upon me. There was a permanent smile on my face that day. My parents were quiet about it, so I predicted a surprise party or something. I was the first person in my immediate family to achieve a traditional four-year bachelor's degree which I was very proud of. It did not matter if my family celebrated my academic achievement because my friends and I were meeting later in East Greenwich for a celebratory dinner and drinks at Twenty Water Street.

Wearing a knee-length silver dress and black patent leather heels, I put on my cap and gown humming the "Pomp and Circumstance" melody to myself as I gazed at the new college graduate in the mirror. My feeling of sheer accomplishment was enormous. It was time to meet my parents who wanted to drive me to my commencement celebration. My college classmates, friends, and I lined up in alphabetical order. We could barely contain our excitement of soon shaking hands with the university President and grabbing the degrees that we had toiled faithfully for. In a short while, I would hear my name called, my major with type of degree, and be handed a beautiful scroll with my professional degree elegantly printed on it, and stamped with the official seal of the University of Rhode Island. Ron, my professor friend, and all of my professors were present cheering all of us on. My grandfather, Aunt Mary, and some of my childhood friends were also in attendance. This would go down in history as one of the happiest moments of my life besides marrying or having children. After we were situated in a huge hall at Keaney Gymnasium in the lower part of campus, it seemed like an eternity before our group was called. We were the human service professionals of the future, everyone including fashion designers, early childhood educators, law enforcement hopefuls, and social workers, to name a few of the career choices in our department. Being bound for a human services profession was, and still is, something to be very proud of. There were a lot of us future teachers, child care directors, economists, and police officers who got our degrees on that hot, humid, spring day in May.

When my name was called, it felt like I was floating up to the stage to grab my degree from the Dean before shaking the university President's hand. I raised it high over my head and loudly yelled, "I did it!" as tears welled up in my eyes. My degree had been earned with the sweat of my brow and five years of living below the poverty line. I had achieved a degree through uncertain time periods throughout my college years when I did not know if I would have a roof over my head or food in my stomach. That day a miracle in my life occurred. I thanked God and modern medicine for letting me live to continue reaching my personal life goals.

After graduating, my classmates and I stood in the corridor taking pictures together. We exchanged numbers and addresses before going our separate ways. My parents left me outside the auditorium for an hour after the graduation ceremony with rain pouring down on me. A classmate stayed with me holding an umbrella over my head cursing my parents for going missing on such an important day of my life. I got a handful of offers for a ride home, even from a local police officer I had grown up with. It was a humiliating situation not knowing if they would pick me up or not. I was the second-to-last person out of thousands to be picked up from the commencement. Not even my parents' impromptu "coffee break" as they called it could get me down on one of the happiest days of my life.

After they drove me back to their house, and I saw the lack of any celebratory planning for their first child's graduation from college, I immediately took my leave. In my opinion, my parents had hit a new low by not having so much as a pizza, cake, or our family, at their home following my college graduation. It felt as though they were not proud of my accomplishment. That was my cue to get ready for the dinner that my closest friends had planned for me. A few moments after returning to my studio apartment, I heard three loud knocks on my door. *Who in the world is that?* I wondered. I was still frustrated by my parents' lack of excitement for higher education on my college graduation day. I miserably asked, "Who is it?" My neighbor Kendra announced herself. She wanted to know how graduation went. Kendra was putting herself through cosmetology school because her parents couldn't accept her lifestyle choices. Her wishing me a happy graduation meant a lot to me.

I heard something in the hallway outside the door and opened it more widely. As I opened the door, I saw Kendra's two roommates with a ton of balloons, *hors d'oeuvres*, drinks, and a huge graduation sheet cake that said, "Congratulations Lara! Class of 1998" on it with some of the most beautiful decorative icing that I had ever seen. Kendra and the guys had really gone "festive" on me just when I needed it. They were some of the best neighbors I have ever had because they were there for me personally. It was wonderful to see them at that moment. We had a great party. We made plans to go to a dance club of my choice in Providence for a night of dancing. I called my other friends from college and work to tell them where to meet us.

It was a fun night at the dance club. My homosexual male neighbors danced to country tunes disregarding any scowls from macho wannabe cowboys. It was exhilarating and humorous to see older club-goers' reactions to our medley of unique friends. All of my friends were quite well-humored and expressive or they would not be close friends of mine. I do not trust people who are too quiet. Quietness too often equated with mental dullness or illness which has never interested me on a friendship level with that type of person. Those with the least to say usually have the most to hide. Kendra and I preferred the hip hop club upstairs. Any dance club with current dance tunes and No Doubt blaring through the speakers was my preference at the time. We danced until they closed, celebrating friendship and my life-changing day together. It was a hedonistic, unforgettable graduation night.

I flew to Clearwater, Florida, for a job interview for the HIV/AIDS case manager position. After being interviewed by the director and the office's case management team, I was called forty-eight hours later. The director wanted me to join their HIV/AIDS team. My answer was a big "Yes." The thought of being able to help men and women diagnosed with HIV and AIDS put a smile of determination upon my face. My elderly caseload was challenging, comfortable, and very rewarding, yet I craved a new challenge. It was time to broaden my horizons and change my latitude. Florida temperatures would be a welcome, warm, change for me. Also, the gulf coast of Florida has some of the most beautiful beaches I have ever seen with talcum powder-soft bright white well-groomed sand. My personal favorite remains Siesta Key Beach which was relatively quiet, yet had plenty of activities for beachgoers. I had one month to put my things in storage and get to the St. Petersburg area near Tampa and Clearwater. Until I received my first paycheck, I would stay with my mother's Aunt Sara, a sweet, no-nonsense, self-made woman who spent thirty years as an administrative assistant with the federal government working for various federal entities including the Environmental Protection Agency and the Pentagon, to name only a few of her interesting assignments. She was a pioneering single mother back when being a single mother was a rare occurrence and highly frowned-upon. She said that co-workers would constantly ask her if she had found a "new husband," yet. She told them one marriage was enough and left it that way. She had a wonderful boyfriend, however, who was "better than a husband" she said, because she could send him home to his place.

When my first paycheck came it didn't amount to two month's

rent at Florida prices in St. Petersburg, so I had to wait two more weeks. It was rough being in someone else's home for thirty days. I paid for half of the utilities and all of my own food because I had overstayed my welcome at Aunt Sara's. I was asked to live with her single recovering alcoholic daughter, a fourth cousin who was not close to me, or closely-related either. There is an old Italian saying, "Houseguests are like fish. They begin to stink after a few days." I did not want that houseguest to be me.

The other issue that came up was this distant cousin's absence of a car or driver's license due to a permanent loss of license related to a DWI conviction that was conveniently left out of conversation with my mother's aunt. I had been duped into helping a single mother pay her bills and chauffeur her misbehaved child around Sarasota County due to his mother's bad behavior years before. In the meantime, I had no time or money with which to secure an apartment. I had to find a way to cut the cousin off and quickly get out of there.

I was pretty angry with my mother who had entrusted me to the wrong people as I started anew in Florida. Didn't she know about these people's serious issues? Why in the world was I being used to help a distant relative meet her daily needs with free babysitting and her own personal taxi service? It was a maddening situation.

My mother had no idea that her aunt would have me live in an impossible situation. Mom felt guilty because her father's side of the family was always distant and had not kept in touch since he passed away when my mother was fifteen. She expected more from her aunt. I expected more out of people who were blood-related. I spent every afternoon and weekend day looking for an apartment. A co-worker of mine advised me on a few apartment complexes on Tampa Bay, near the Tropicana Stadium in old St. Petersburg. The only place that I could afford after being tapped financially by a trashy cousin was a tiny apartment in the attic of an old house. It had a crude bathroom that was inconveniently located in the kitchen area. There was a tiny bathtub with a hand-held shower next to the kitchen cabinets. There was a tiny living area with enough room for a small chair and television. There was a slightly-raised carpeted loft big enough for a small futon bed. The landlady knew I was desperate for a roof over my head. She rushed me into signing the lease paperwork, knowing full well that I was less-than-satisfied with the accommodations but could afford nothing better. Immediately after I had signed the lease to make my stay official, several large cockroaches appeared on the carpeted stairs leading up to my disgusting sleeping area. On a positive note, the cockroaches were better to live with than the blood-related leech I had been staying with. It was my first, albeit disgusting, Florida abode.

My case management position had very low income potential as it was an annual position renewed by the Ryan White Foundation with funds that changed according to fundraising levels and matching federal funds. I had relocated to an area with inflated tourist prices on everything including fuel, food, and living accommodations. The job was excellent, so I made due in order to stay at the agency. I had taken the job to help keep men and women alive, not to become a millionaire, although affluent locals informed me that one or two million didn't hurt when living in the high-rent, gorgeous neighborhood near the yacht club.

My clients ranged in age from barely eighteen to sixty-something. The men and women on my caseload were from all walks of life. The AIDS virus is not exclusive to skid row drug addicts or highly-promiscuous homosexual men as in the rumors America's homophobes all too commonly propagate about how the disease is contracted. For example, I was in the military with a pleasant young mother of two who had gotten HIV from her husband who had cheated on her with an infected prostitute while on duty in a foreign country. He broke his wedding vows many times over and two little boys would soon be motherless. More than a third of new HIV cases since 2005 have been through heterosexual intercourse. It is sad that many Americans have no idea how a person becomes infected, or care to learn about this horrible worldwide epidemic that affects approximately 1.2 million Americans and over 33.2 million men, women, and children worldwide (www.unaids.org, www.who.int). Approximately two-and-a-half million of the world's children in 2007 who tested positive for HIV. Around three hundred and thirty thousand children died in 2007 from AIDS. In Africa, alone, there are twelve million orphans whose parent or parents died of AIDS (www.avert.org).

In Florida, and I believe this is the case elsewhere, I encountered men and women who were mostly deceived by unfaithful partners, spouses, or a drug-using partner who shared a needle when doing drugs. One of my clients claimed to have been infected during a rape by a mentally-ill HIV-infected man who said he wanted to "get as many gay guys as possible" because he claimed to hate them, although it was a mystery how he had contracted the disease himself. That was one of the more gruesome infection contraction histories.

Each of my clients had a unique story to tell as to how he or she had gotten the disease. Several were parents. Some had small children who had no idea that Mommy or Daddy could be dying. Luckily, most of my female clients had contracted HIV after giving birth to their child or children. Unfortunately, these children would have to deal with a very ill parent, or with losing their parent, in the future whenever the virus decided not to be restrained by medication or the immune system. This usually happened when a client's (Please do not erase T-cell because it is the common term for the blood cells that fight HIV. Thank you.) CD-4T- or T-cell count went to two hundred or below, which is considered the AIDS infection level. An uninfected person has a TT-cell count of between 600 to 1500 cells/mm3 (www.hhs.gov). When a client's TT-cell count fell below 500 cells, he or she was qualified to receive counseling and HIV-AIDS-related assistance through our agency. Our goal was to help clients to keep up with their daily responsibilities, monitor their viral loads, and help to keep their immune systems stronger through helping to better afford their various expensive medications.

AZT, or Azidothymidine, is the antiretroviral drug of choice for many who are infected, but does not work for every infected person. Magic Johnson is the exception, not the rule. Although not a scientist, I found among my cases that many clients who were very physically fit and between eighteen and below middle-age seemed to go symptom free with the appropriate drug cocktail. Those previously in poor health, or who had the disease detected too late for some drugs to work, tended to become ill more quickly. Their immune systems were not strong enough to fight this destructive, powerful disease.

My job was to check my clients' T-cell counts, make sure that each client was on top of their lab testing, and taking their medication as directed. Another duty of the position was to get discounted HIV/AIDS inhibitor drugs to low-income clients. I also coordinated with other social service agencies to make sure that my clients had everything they needed to stay as safe and healthy as possible. I encouraged my more introverted clients to attend support groups at the main office where my office was located. I told them to say "hello" to me so I could track their social progress as a participant in a therapy sessions. Some of my clients came by to say "hello" to me on a regular basis which was a highlight of any office day. Several of my gay, straight, male, female, and transgender clients were financially stable, or in some cases quite wealthy, and preferred to meet with me over lunch.

I enjoyed those working lunches. My clients could count on me for casual conversation once the questionnaire was complete and the latest copy of these clients' lab results were in my hot little hands. These people were slowly fading or successfully fighting the infection. Most of my clients had such full calendars that most non-infected folks would be hard-pressed to keep up with them. Many of my clients went to events or participated in activities or hobbies that made them happy. Many of my clients seemed to know that happiness can keep a person alive longer than despair can. Giving up gave the AIDS monster the upper hand, so they had to live life to the fullest in spite of their infections. I deeply admired their determination to stay healthy and happy. All people should live life as though each day could be their last. There would be a lot less bitter people walking this planet. Happiness can keep you alive longer or make every day better that you are here fighting your illness.

The home visits were often interesting, sometimes alarming, and mostly enjoyable. One client was dating a millionaire interior designer whose townhouse was like a personal five-star hotel, minus the mini fridge, with automatic everything and some of the most beautiful original artwork that I had ever seen in a private residence. They had mint condition antique furniture with some newer pieces. Each room was colorful with bright rich silks, chiffon, and toile throughout. He served us iced tea with a ra eal silver service that had to be French with ornate *fleurs de lis* etched onto the grand handles. He had excellent classical music or operas playing during the entire visit. His favorite popular vocalists were Elton John and Celine Dion. His home was always a vacation for the senses. Great smells, an ocean view, and excellent music were the standard.

Another home visit was to a gentleman's home which had both gay and straight icons of the art, music, and cinema genres. I absolutely loved his Marilyn Monroe and Bette Davis photographs and prints throughout his home. He was an accomplished artist. His art was photography. His portfolio was extensive and impressive. On a table in his living room, there was a gorgeous photo of his mother that he had taken. She had been very supportive of him and his lifestyle. His partner had passed on, but he made a lot of friends who were there when he needed them through the support group and art community. I went to one of the art walks there to see him in action. I looked forward to visiting him. He always had a new piece of pop art or photography to show me. When I asked him if he was becoming depressed he said, "Hey honey. I have my ruby slippers in my closet if I ever get too sick from the big 'A.' Until then, I'm going to live it up." Visiting him was so enjoyable because he shared his knowledge of the photography and art worlds with me. He was a happy, kind, and determined soul.

My supervisor was a very cheerful, hard-charging married mother in her forties who had a heart of gold. She shared her wisdom related to the different clients' home situations. We went together to a handful of clients whom she considered to be tough cases. Two that we visited together were an ex-convict and former prostitute. My ex-convict had been a heroine user and dealer who had a run-in with an infected needle and not long afterward with the law. My gut told me that he was far from being a monster. All things considered, he had a history of violent behavior in his past so I had to talk with him at the front door with my supervisor. Drugs definitely ruin lives more often than not. His story was evidence that hard drugs can change people for the worse. He had an important story to tell but too often men and women like him are stigmatized and never allowed to tell their stories, especially to those who need to hear the warnings the most, our country's often overly-impressionable teens.

My former prostitute was a gorgeous, young, long-haired copper-tanned woman in her early twenties who used prostitution to put food on the table for her aging grandparents and three children. Now living in poverty without income from her former self-destructive occupation, she was adjusting to clean living while her insides were fighting the most murderous escort of them all. Although living in squalor, her parents were very kind people, refusing to cave in to ugly bitterness over their daughter's situation. She had a baby who also had the virus, a beautiful baby girl walking around in a diaper with a bright pink pacifier in her mouth. She proudly took her baby steps completely unaware of how her life would be so different and potentially much shorter than most American children. When you meet an infant or toddler with HIV, it upsets you that to this day no vaccine exists to protect babies, or the rest of humankind, from contracting AIDS.

My supervisor let me in on her tools of the trade for dealing with difficult clients. She told me to always double up for visits to clients with criminal pasts or dangerous living situations. She also recommended a police escort for suspected criminal activity in a client's home. I followed her advice and worked without incident. Her advice was sage and I turned to her often for her wisdom.

My co-workers, too, were excellent resources for any questions that I had about certain client situations or medical clarification on lab results. My co-workers at Jewish family services were an invigoratingly diverse group. Estrella, one of my co-workers who was Cuban, was studying for the U.S. citizenship test. She was middle-aged and tough as nails. She was very serious about her job and difficult to pry from her paperwork or telephone to answer any questions. She had all she could stand on her plate, which I could empathize with.

Another female co-worker was Tamika, a glamorous African American young woman in her mid-twenties. She had onyx, silken chin-length hair and a keen sense of style. She and I became the office fashionistas. We were tough, trendy, intelligent, and never went to work without interesting clothes, hair, and make-up. The other female case manager, Kaylea, that I worked with was a forty-five-year-old lesbian who had an unwavering devotion to every client, sharp wit, a pixie hairstyle, and who was an earth mother-type on a mission. Her biting liberal feminist sense of humor was an interesting contrast to a few ultra-conservative women who worked there. Some of the women in the office were obsessed with futilely trying to convert their clients to whatever religious affiliation they were members of, in an oftentimes overtly religious, and mostly unsuccessful, manner. Kaylea had an amazing way of making me laugh about issues that were usually very depressing if I couldn't find a humorous release. I really liked her cutting edge humor and her huge heart. She was magical in her ability to transform the most uncooperative client into an informative self-advocate within minutes using a few authoritative words and barrier-breaking humor.

My favorite co-worker there was Jonas, my mysterious co-worker who spoke little of his personal life and more about his clients. He was beyond handsome, brawny, metrosexual, and a triathlete who had competed nationally for the past several years. Jonas had eyes the color of the Gulf coast water at midday, a stop-you-in-your-tracks blue. He and I became fast friends. His personality attracted me like steel to my strong magnetic field. Kaylea had too much of a rough edge for me at times since I was little Miss Optimistic. Our conversations were mostly limited to discussions of particular clients and recommendations for venues that her "hetero" friends enjoyed. She was sweet under that rock hard exterior.

I consider myself jade-proof, so Jonas was my upbeat co-worker of choice. He too liked my Sarah Jessica Parker from *Sex and the City* wardrobe. I can mix and match with the best of them. Jonas took me under his wing. We both had cheerful outlooks on life which allowed for lengthy exchanges about our cases and finding fun outside of the office. Jonas drove a Jeep Wrangler which was a very breezy, hip ride in the summer heat of the Tampa suburbs. He shared his favorite spots for eating, drinking, and making merry. We had similar musical tastes, hip hop, pop, and house music. Like me, Jonas liked his music loud and high energy. He was a co-worker who I could vent to and have a blast with. We would laugh at the most ridiculous songs because we had stressful jobs that required over the top releases of a lot of frustration. It took a lot of good music, support from friends, and humor to hold back the tears on days when the HIV/AIDS killer overcame another victim.

I received the nickname "Sarah Jessica," for the character Carrie in *Sex and the City*, because I wore oftentimes loud, cheerfully bright, quirky clothing to the office. None of my outfits were too racy, although some were noted as too loud or just plain edgy on the style. My theory has always been to do things my way, no matter what the status quo of the moment dictates. If style becomes rigid and too conformist, then it is no longer style. Fashion then becomes a lot of people blindly and unoriginally following a trend. It is always better to lead than to follow. It is always more risky to be a leader, but I prefer the uncharted terrain and rough roads in life that leaders are drawn to.

Every day, the office manager would say, "Okay, Sarah Jessica, let's see the outfit." I would so my best fashion model imitation by doing a few sashays. Rotating around in a slow circle, I did my best to portray a truly Carrie-esque Sarah Jessica moment. She would clap from behind the doctor's office open glass window and tell me what she liked best about my ensemble of the day. She was a happily-married woman who got a kick out of my bold, shameless attitude. I decided that since I was helping men and women with a deadly virus I had better be cheerful and gleefully-wardrobed each workday. If I were very ill, I would quit a depressing case manager like a bad habit. It was our job to be realistic and strong, making whatever time clients had left on this planet as productive and healthy as possible, period. That was what I hoped to bring to each visit. Hopefulness, strength, and cheer can go a long way in the life of the chronically ill or oppressed.

Jonas asked me out for dinner and a movie. I thought that was a very nice gesture on his part. Who wouldn't want to go out on the town with such a caring, fun-loving, not to mention totally hard-bodied, beyond-good-looking man? As we quickly approached Friday night's festivities, I noticed a photo of Jonas and someone who looked like his brother at a café. I said, "Your brother is very handsome. It must run in the family." Kaylea overheard, her witchy laugh echoing across from the far corner of the office that the two shared. Jonas turned bright red and explained, "No, he isn't related. He is gay and so am I. That is my partner Len. We were eating lunch at one of our favorite restaurants." I was very surprised. This was the strangest expose of the most undetectably-homosexual man that I had ever met. He was handsome, manly, athletic, straight-in-every-way-but-one and had fallen in love with two women in both high school and college. Alas, my new friend and co-worker was indisputably gay and I had about two seconds to get over my lack of lifestyle detection ability. My gaydar had malfunctioned. The pressure was indisputably off as far as any office romance was concerned.

I went out with Jonas and his partner Len to a movie and dinner. I never felt like a third wheel. We three had a few great nights on the town. I was respected as a good friend. Jonas and his partner were very honest with me about relationships with clients, my excellent job performance, and my appearance. When a gay man tells you that you are beautiful, it is much more believable than the same compliment from a straight man who may have an ulterior motive. God bless my gay male friends for being so accepting of me and always being honest about my appearance, for better or worse. Their favorite weekend establishments had much better music than most of the clubs in the area. It is not always easy to find clubs with a great crowd, adrenaline-inciting dance beats, international music, and video screens unless you are vacationing in Las Vegas, Nevada.

Jonas would ask me to apartment- and dog-sit on weekends that he and Len went out of town. One day, when I was house-sitting I got hungry. There was a banana in Jonas's fruit bowl. The banana was a plastic deadringer for the real deal, but what was hidden beneath it was the real shocker. There was a blue-labeled medicine bottle with Jonas's name upon it with the letters AZT stamped on it. My first good friend here in Florida was, like his clients, HIV-positive. After collapsing into his retro leopard-spotted chair, I began to bawl. Not many times in my life have I sobbed spontaneously, but this "too much information" moment floored me. I was also very angry. Jonas was not some drug abuser, nor was he irresponsible. Jonas was one of the smartest social workers I had ever worked with or befriended. How did such a sensible person get HIV? I knew the answer to this question, but in my anger asked it out loud anyway. I held Jonas's adorable male Jack Russell terrier and slept on his couch where they found me the next day.

I confronted him telling him that I did not feel sorry for him. I demanded to know how he got it, or rather who he had gotten it from, in order to better understand his prognosis. He did not want me to feel sad for him. He didn't tell me because he felt that his HIV-positive status would overshadow our friendship. I told him that it was ridiculous to think that I would feel sorry for him. I felt helpless and angry because there was nothing that I could do to help him get rid of the incurable life threatening disease that would little-by-little try to kill his body's internal defense mechanisms. As you know, when a friend or family member has a life-threatening illness, you get very angry. When you stop being angry, you have to do whatever you can to enjoy every second that you have left with your beloved partner, family member, or friend.

*Chapter Twelve*

## Changing Gear with a Different Career

The expensive, yet quaint, St. Petersburg lifestyle did not quite jibe with my roach-infested studio apartment with the toilet in the kitchen. There were so many bugs in the apartment that I could not sleep well at night. It just wasn't working for me and I cannot stand feeling defeated. After several months, I decided to head back to New England to cool off and try to get my old job back. Jonas knew that our agency was not paying well, so he helped me pack my things to head back to New England. I loved Florida, but needed a few more years under my belt professionally to afford a decent place to live and to command a higher salary. My trip back to New England occurred on Fourth of July weekend. There was nothing but gridlock on the narrow Route 95 throughout the deep south. It was a pretty drive, however. If you ever want star treatment down south, just meander several miles off of the 95 and find a small southern town. There is a slower pace; and who does not like being called such sweet things as "sweetie pie" and "sugar" when you are at a Piggly Wiggly or a local restaurant? I just had to get back to what was familiar until I worked my way up and paid down my college debt. Nothing is worse to me than to watch Fourth of July fireworks on a cheap television set at the Economotel. It was miserable. I missed my clients, new friends, and my independence already in a day's time. My decision to return to Rhode Island came when my living conditions became worse in Florida than at any other point in my life. This Independence Day symbolized the weekend trip back to dependence on family which I was not too thrilled about. To make a long story short, my previous employer did not rehire me. The living situation with my parents was unlivable because I required more privacy and personal space than they were willing to give. Last, but not least, the case manager position at a retirement community in northern Rhode Island was relaxing, but not the best fit for my high energy. I longed to get back to working with children, especially teenagers.

It was time for a career change. The next chapter of my life would involve teaching. I made a decision to research climate, salaries, and cost of living of the southern and western U.S. because the economy in Rhode Island was at a standstill. I was unwilling to simply spin my wheels in one place while the rest of the country, and my former college classmates, seemed to be moving forward. With considerable medical costs to consider and college loans to pay back, California on a beginning teacher's salary was very desirable, yet too expensive.

Texas had George W. Bush for governor who had liquidated the English language learner programs in the state, therefore teachers had to speak Spanish or, as one principal said, "you had better forget teaching here without being fluent in Spanish because Governor Bush made ELL programs extinct." Most of the southeastern states had beginning salaries in the low 20s which was unacceptable for me with my monthly loan payments. I also needed healthcare benefits, so a typical substitute teacher position was out of the question. I had to find a teaching position for a full-time long-term substitute that included good pay and benefits. The only teaching position offered in Rhode Island was a substitute position for K-through-12 for the North Kingstown school district. This position had no benefits, nor would I be accruing retirement points. I had learned a valuable lesson about spreading myself too thin years earlier. After some careful thinking, I turned down the North Kingstown job.

There was one state that had long-term substitute positions with livable wages, retirement points, a low cost of living, and health benefits which was a perfect fit for me at the time. The teaching position was in the Grand Canyon State. I knew that moving to Arizona had its risks. I had been placed on the waiting list for a state case management position with a starting salary in the mid-40s with full state-paid benefits, excellent retirement benefits, and the bonus of a state-provided work vehicle. It was a Rhode Island social worker's dream to have a coveted state position. It had been three years since I had taken and aced the state social work exam. My intuition told me that I would probably not be receiving any magic phone call or correspondence anytime soon.

After considering all of my options as a single college graduate who was more adventurous than your average young woman, I was off to the Wild West and to my new career choice of elementary school teacher. My first memory of Arizona was the drive out of the Sky Harbor Airport in Tempe which, as I was quickly corrected, is pronounced Tem-pee. There were flowering cacti everywhere with pink, white, and fuchsia blossoms upon them. On the drive to Florence, we drove through an army of saguaro cacti with their immense height, solid torsos, and thick waving twisted limbs reaching upward to the light blue sunny sky. They were a beautiful bright green. I had landed in a different world, it seemed. This alternate universe had a desert sea of sandstone-colored dust and bright sand in the place of green grass, coastline, and Atlantic Ocean. The sun was much hotter than in New England. After ten minutes in the dessert, my face was bright red from sunburn. Back east that kind of sunburn only happened due to boating, swimming, or skiing without wearing sun block. In the desert, you get sunburn in spite of your sun block of choice if you stay outside longer than the recommended time that the meteorologists suggest on any given day.

After meeting with the very kind special education director, a decision was made to invite me to take over an 8th grade special education class. The position was full-time with benefits for the remainder of the school year, January through May with no guarantee of being hired for the following school year. That was the main element of uncertainty regarding the position. The position required taking mildly learning-challenged children out of the general middle school classroom for structured core subject instruction according to each student's IEP, or Individual Education Plan. The director and principal felt that my years working with at-risk teens had prepared me for the middle school teaching position they were offering. I told the director that I would need a week to make a decision. She granted me one week and a guest room at her home until my first paycheck came in. Unlike Florida, I would have enough money to make rent and loan payments each month.

After thinking about it long and hard for a week, I decided to take the Arizona job. Although it would be a difficult teaching assignment, I knew I was tough enough and a good listener. With the proper tools and on-the-job mentoring I believed that I would succeed. My classroom would have a bilingual assistant to help me communicate with Spanish speakers. The school's principal gave me thirty days to get my affairs in order and move out to Casa Nuevo.

My personal belongings were stored in a friend-of-a-friend's basement for retrieval at a later date. I packed everything except the kitchen sink into my extremely compact two-door forest green sports coupe. I must have looked ridiculous with all of my belongings piled to the ceiling of my little car. This was one of the most courageous endeavors of my life, to once again leave all that was familiar in Rhode Island for the unknown folklore-rich southwestern United States. As a Generation X pioneer of the new twenty-first century, I left New England's high cost of living for a one bedroom apartment with a community pool and hot tub a few paces from my front door. My life was changing dramatically for the better financially, aesthetically, and professionally. For some of my friends who "stuck it out" in New England, my moving away was an oddity. The move was considered by some as too large of a personal risk with too many unknowns. For me, it was a way out of poverty-level wages and one room studio apartments. Those were items I would not miss at all. The economy in Rhode Island had been at a virtual standstill since the early nineties and not much had changed by the year two thousand. The main problem was the large number of us twenty-something college graduates interviewing for the same small number of good jobs throughout the smallest state in the union.

It did not matter how intelligent you were or where you had gone to college. The waiting period for a challenging, excellent-paying job with benefits was the same for everyone. Not many of the "townies" that I grew up with in our small rural coastal New England community stayed there. Most of us got out of there via out-of-state work, college, the Peace Corps, or the military. We went to find work elsewhere to keep our heads above water financially and to forge independence from our parents who never wanted to see us move away. My parents are still disappointed with how neither my brother nor I work or live in the area where we grew up. The local economy was hard on young people. The thought of bringing up children where they could barely afford the rent was unrealistic and dismal for many of my childhood friends.

I go back to visit my family once or twice annually for at least a week to try to catch up with everyone. Whenever I return, I am guaranteed a warm, familiar welcome as a former "townie" by the locals I was fortunate to grow up among. The folks that comprise Charlestown, Rhode Island, are an eccentric, nature-loving, hard-working bunch who live along the beautiful Southern New England Atlantic coast. It is not a glamorous town, but it has a very strong, self-confident, and stable identity. We were raised in a quiet, rural community where our safety was paramount and neighbors looked after one another's family members, property, and animals. We went to excellent public schools where teachers were paid well and never lacked quality classroom resources. My mother and father never complained about the taxes because education, safety, and stability were crucial to their children's futures. We were fortunate not to attend inadequately-funded schools where the teachers looked forlorn and were frustrated as they do in too many communities in our country today.

Arizona's public education funding was the lowest in the country in the year two thousand and has been battling for better education funding ever since. A destructive Republican extreme right wing state legislative majority has been shortchanging Arizona's children, college students, and educators for approximately thirty years. Not even the popular Democratic governor, Janet Napolitano, could do much to change the state budget to improve Arizona's schools. My hope is that the state constitution will be rewritten to mandate a functional level of educational funding that keeps up with Arizona's population growth and needs of its student population. Our nation's children deserve top notch educations that will make them competitive locally and globally. Until much of the leadership in Arizona's state government becomes pro-education, the children there will continue to be left with underdeveloped intellectual capital. Not only this, but excellent learning environments do not include overcrowded classrooms where educators struggle to teach every child equally, where classroom resources are scarce, and cultural exploration is often difficult to attain for the students due to budget constraints.

Immediately after moving to Arizona from Rhode Island, I received my first graduated college loan invoice for more money than my new teaching salary would cover. Since my salary left me short on other necessary living expenses, I searched for a part-time job somewhere in the new city that I was an official inhabitant of. There were no part-time jobs in social work or education in Casa Nuevo, so I applied at every respectable bar and restaurant in the city. About a week after I had applied, I got a phone call from a manager at a popular local watering hole near the main highway called Uncle Sam's. The female manager, "TJ," explained that she was offering a high-paying bartending position with the potential to become Uncle Sam's assistant manager if I could bolster the number of regulars, increase restaurant profit, and keep the restaurant running smoothly. My co-workers were a diverse, festive bunch. We worked very well as a team, never carelessly criticizing each other, and helped each other with our duties. It wasn't easy working until 3 a.m. on a Friday night when I had already worked that day at the middle school, but my job at Sam's was a wonderful change of scenery and pace from the school which was what I needed, especially as the teacher of special needs children.

My new part-time job as a bartender and closer allowed me to act my age and use my management skills in a way that got me noticed by the restaurant's owner. After one month, I became assistant manager, working five nights and weekend days with a pay raise included in the job upgrade. I was grossing weekly what most of the teachers made in two weeks. My energy levels were such that I breezed through both jobs without much ado. Whatever lack of excitement or school politics had occurred during the day in the one-horse city, my night life whisked me away after only a few moments behind the bar. Regulars liked me to sing karaoke while I poured the drinks and popped the tops on their beer bottles. One of my favorite songs to sing was Reba McEntire's "Fancy." Another favorite was the funny disco song, "Kung Fu Fighting" from the days when Bruce Lee was the Saturday morning King of Television. My song choices depended on my customer's requests and whatever mood I was in. My favorite part of my job duties was conversing with my regulars about their lives. I have always worn an "S" for social worker on my forehead. It was exhilarating to listen, give advice to those who wanted it, or to simply make light of a serious situation in one of their lives. In return I got excellent tips and insider information on the goings-on of the small city.

Every night I would enjoy a night cap with whoever was still at the bar before I cleared the place and balanced the books in the back office. My preference was always an ice cold strawberry daiquiri or a Kahlua and milk. Then, it was off to the back office to do the daily bookkeeping. It was a great job for a social butterfly who needed an escape from the daily "new teacher" grind.

A few months into the contract year, I could see that I would not be seeking a new contract with that particular school district. The administration bordered on corrupt. The married principal was having a very public affair with the, no-pun-intended, physical education teacher. A social studies teacher who was also the girls' soccer coach was caught looking at pornography in class with students present. His wife was a Casa Nuevo city employee and his highly-inappropriate perversions were apparently being overlooked. The math teacher was burnt out and ready for retirement. She was visibly uncomfortable around the vibrant young men and women that she taught. The three excellent, by contrast teachers of math, science, and social studies on my teaching team made my assignment bearable since the school's morale couldn't get much lower or it would have failed to exist.

*Chapter Twelve + One*

**Somebody notices that I have the best tools for success in life and love.**

My social life on the weekends made up for my very busy work life during the week. Whenever I could get a weekend night off, which was rare, some fellow teachers and I went out for dinner, drinks, dancing, or karaoke. Sometimes we just went out to dinner and then out to dance. One night we went to one of our favorite carousing venues, the Draft House, in the Arizona State University college town of Tempe for ice cold drinks and high-energy dancing to a medley of music genres. This is where I would meet someone who would change my life.

The only married person in our group was talking to a man who looked around my age at the table we had claimed for our night's revelry. *Who is this man? How dare he cramp our single women styles with his lingering?* The only thing to do was to ask my co-worker's friend who she was talking to. It was her brother Scott. He stopped by to discuss some family matter. I abruptly asked, "What are you doing hanging out with us on a Friday night?" He politely answered, "I decided to grab a beer, chat with my sister, and relax for a few minutes. How about you?" I didn't know how to take his calm demeanor; therefore I explained how on my infrequent girls' nights out I enjoyed a friendly crowd and dancing. I added that, if he stuck around, men might think we were an item and wouldn't ask me to dance. He assured me that he would keep his distance since he wasn't much of a dancer and simply told me to "have fun." *"That is generous of you,"* I thought, annoyed by his insistent presence during our girls' night out. *What part of 'girl' in "girls' night out" didn't he understand?*

Sometimes, when you are single, you just want to keep all prospects at a safe distance. This Scott individual had overstayed his welcome and was too close to me for comfort. He kept giving me compliments about my dancing and my selection of black fishnet pantyhose. Fishnet pantyhose were, as I recall, very "in" during the first few months of the year 2000. I didn't let him slow me down. Every time a potential dance partner would ask me to dance, I went off without hesitation, hoping that he would be turned off enough to move on. Much to my aggravation he stayed. Each time that I returned to the table to cool off from my dancing binge, sip my drink, and reload the lip color, Scott would tell me exactly how long it took for each dance partner to ask me for a dance. Like some Friday night B. F. Skinner quantifying dance partner requests he stated, "You're down to twenty seconds and that's going to be hard to beat." Then he had the audacity to laugh mischievously, which offended me because he had caught me off-guard.

*Why is he tracking me?* Besides, I wasn't that interested. He didn't even dance. He was wearing a baseball cap, wasn't stylishly dressed, and was actually a complete fashion victim that night. My type of man was boisterous, smooth, bold, buff, and had a keen sense of style. This man was handsome, had eyes that were as deep blue as the Atlantic Ocean, but needed help in the self-expression area, at least where women were concerned. I had no patience for men who were not self-starters.

It was time to see what he was made of. I obstinately demanded, "Are you going to keep track of my dance partners or are you going to dance with me?" He answered with the following question: "Would you like to dance the next slow song with me?

I am not much of a dancer." I gave it right back to him by replying, "I thought you'd never ask." He grabbed my hand to lead me to the dance floor. As we stepped on the wooden dance floor a popular country love song, "Amazed" by Lonestar, began to play: "Every time our eyes meet, this feeling inside me, is more than I can take..." Scott and I had been dancing an arm's length apart when he pulled me closer to him. He held me close enough for me to feel his breath on my ear and neck. It was in that moment when he held me close that I knew he was "the one." I looked straight at him, this stranger who waltzed uninvited into my single womanhood. I thanked God for sending me "the one," my soulmate. That night ended up being my best girls' night out.

Scott and I became inseparable, instant best friends who both had strong family values and similar upbringings, and who enjoyed both work and play equally. He was the first man who had me even considering marriage as a relationship option. I had been unmarried since age eighteen and I was now twenty-eight years old being bitten by a marriage bug that had overlooked me until then. It took me a decade beyond eighteen to meet a man strong and sensitive enough for me to consider saying, "I do." The only problem was that Scott wasn't ready for a soulmate, much less marriage, a concept that he was all-too-familiar with. His first marriage had been a disaster. He was a thirty-one-year-old divorced single father of a nine-year-old boy.

His son had some hang-ups regarding female authority figures in his life, so let's say his reception of me was a bit chilly. With a mother who was unavailable physically and emotionally most of the time, what was this new woman his father was dating going to do to improve his daily life? When Scott and I first began dating, it was refreshing, but not without turmoil in regard to Scott's son's overprotective mother, Scott's needy ex-wife, and this little boy who was unwilling to share his father with anyone else. Scott's dating life had been nonexistent due to an over-involved immediate family, therefore I insisted that we do things on our own and with his son as soon as we were agreed that marriage might be in our future. After a year and not much progress in terms of his pledge of a serious commitment, I employed my rule of not wasting time on any man and decided to break up with him. He had too many hang-ups regarding relationships. I would not be used as entertainment to brighten his off time from managing his transit company in Scottsdale. I searched for a teaching job somewhere in Arizona away from Scott and his apprehensiveness. After scanning the Arizona Republic for weeks while still bartending at Uncle Sam's, I found an excellent teaching help-wanted ad. The listing read, "Certified Elementary teacher needed for Havasupai Reservation Elementary School, Supai, AZ. Contact Mr. Argus at 222-555-3454." I looked up Supai, Arizona on www.mapquest.com to find that the reservation was located on a remote Native American Reservation at the bottom of the Grand Canyon. It was perfect!

Scott wanted some space. He was about to have hundreds of miles of it between us. I was ready to distance myself from Scott in order to let him ponder a life without me in the picture. Having been brought up in a rural community, I longed for a small-town environment, for the rural life, and to be one with nature again. City life had been wearing on me. Maybe this teaching position would lead to something long-term. I was ready for a new challenge and had always felt a sense of service to Native Americans because of our country's historically ill treatment of their people. It was thrilling to think that I could do my part to help right a historical wrong. I would do this by helping to provide the children there an excellent culturally-sensitive American public education that many in our country take for granted. My adventurous spirit was piqued. I applied immediately. Several weeks later, I received a call from Agnes Champlain, the tribal council president. She was calling to ask me to an interview. She sent me elaborate directions to the south rim of the Grand Canyon's Hualapai Hilltop where I would take a helicopter to the reservation eight miles inward on the sandy rust-colored canyon floor. Scott was not as happy for me as I had hoped. We broke up on friendly terms while he said he wanted more than friendship. Refusing his affection was an unwelcome form of self-torture that would be impossible to get used to. I had fallen in love with him. I had to get far away from him to get over my feelings for him. If Scott changed his mind about our relationship getting more serious, he would have to prove it. If I was offered the reservation teaching job, he would have to drive four hours, catch a horse, fly in a helicopter, or hike eight or more miles to see me.

The intense interview with the tribal council was an hour long. Agnes was obviously the person who had the most interest in my possible employment. She was a very pretty middle-aged woman with gorgeous bright brown eyes and blue-black hair, petite and thin with a resemblance to Loretta Lynn, only with olive skin. I liked her immediately. She was very forthcoming on her marriage to a white Protestant minister which she said was quite a scandal at the time. Tribal leader's daughters did not marry white men "back then," she said with a smile.

The other tribal men and women questioned me with hypothetical situations regarding the isolation of the reservation. Could I handle extended time on the reservation during a winter storm period? Could I handle time away from modern life? Was I prepared to immerse myself in a culture that had survived thousands of years at the Grand Canyon and Flagstaff, Arizona? Was I ready to teach the children while integrating Native American history and the Supai culture into daily lessons? I knew that I was strong enough to meet these challenges and therefore answered in the affirmative to all questions. Mail came by Pony Express, the last surviving route of its kind in the United States. There was no internet, although Bill Gates and his wife had visited the reservation in the past citing a great need for tribal internet access. The newspaper would come two to three days late, depending on the day, due to coordination with the U.S. mail service mule and horse runs. The most current news came from the radio, I would teach fourth and fifth grade, combined, with a Supai teaching assistant to speak to the children in their native language, if offered the position. As an avid American history buff, lover of nature, and an adventurous person, I looked forward to the opportunity to envelope myself within this beautiful place, the home of the Havasupai tribe. Havasupai means "the people of the blue-green water." To see this place is to visit a type of natural paradise south of the Colorado River in the southwestern United States. It was home to the exotic Havasu, Mooney, Beaver, and Navajo Falls. I got to see all except the Beaver Falls on the day of my interview with the help of a tribal guide. He shared with us various Havasupai historical facts and how the falls got their names. He told us about the flora and fauna in great detail. He warned us about a beautiful hallucinogenic night-blooming moonflower that, in small amounts, could cause a person to hallucinate, but any greater amount could make that person insane or poison him to death. He said many a human and animal had succumbed to the flowering shrub. Some survived and some did not. Those who did not heed the tribe's warnings sometimes ended up dead in this beautiful place. We were warned about not hiking alone. We were warned that flood waters became deep and strong very quickly, and that hiking or horseback riding in ice or snow was what he termed "suicidal." With a sense of humor and a wry grin he commented, "Some people like to live dangerously, but the Creator is stronger than a human or animal and therefore nature always wins." I am happy that this tribal historian had shared the tribe's basic history, climate, and other important cultural information with us.

The Havasupai tribe has painstakingly retained their native language. It was plain to see that this tribe maintained its unique culture regardless of the modern world "up top" away from the reservation. No guns or liquor were allowed on the reservation due to past serious problems with both. I was, and still am, impressed by the tribe's historical and cultural integrity. Their desire to retain their cultural heritage is paramount and trumps the reservation concept that was developed to erase Native American influence and culture through oppressive laws and demands of the Anglos during the not-so-distant pioneer days in Arizona.

The Havasupai are a peaceful tribe that had to trick the Apaches into leaving them alone at the bottom of the canyon many moons ago. They outsmarted Geronimo without much resistance, which says a lot about the tremendous negotiation skills of the tribal members. Unlike many Native American tribes, this tribe refused to cave when the United States government tried to kick them out of the Grand Canyon many decades ago. Tribal leaders said "No," and refused to budge. The triumphant evidence of their successful negotiations with the federal government, then and now, is a thriving reservation with every intention to survive in a rapidly-changing American nation, a nation whose mainstream culture embraces modernism. The Havasupai rely on tourism for their main source of income as has been the case since the early 1980s. There was a well-kept lodge, a small hotel, and a large picturesque campground in close proximity to Mooney and Havasu Falls. The campground consists of beautiful grassy campsites with large sturdy picnic tables along the gorgeous blue-green tinted rapidly-flowing creek.

The Havasupai keep a safe distance from modern America, believing that its influence is unhealthy for the tribe's children and the preservation of their culture. Many immigrants to this country have cited the same phenomenon. To remain strong as a culture, tribal members had to continue fighting to save their people and culture from becoming a mere memory. Preserving a culture as old as theirs takes perseverance and a lot of legal maneuvering which the Supai are native champions at. They always come together in a crisis and always have. I admired their rebel spirit which was encased in a rich history of a tight-knit tribal community, enduring self-sufficiency, and steadfast preservation of all things Havasupai.

On the day I interviewed, I met other teachers who were interviewing for jobs. There was Native American preference only for those who were already certified to teach in Arizona. After the interviews, there were only a few of us, myself included, who were qualified to teach at the school and were confident about our employment prospects. It was time to eat a meal at the tribe's café. I had the best Indian taco of my lifetime on the sweetest Indian fry bread topped with delicious seasoned cooked kidney beans with fresh mixed grated cheese, tomatoes, and lettuce. Just thinking about those Indian tacos makes my mouth water. While I waited for the last helicopter out of the canyon, I noticed families all around me waiting for loved ones who were coming in on the chopper that I waited for. One of the mothers used a traditional papoose for her baby. I asked her how her infant handled being confined to one spot for so long. She answered that being in a papoose calms the baby and improves temperament. She also cited that having him in a papoose allowed her to walk for long periods of time with her son safely bound to the cradle board. Her son was a tiny adorable butterfly in his infancy cocoon. He didn't seem to mind his anti-modern baby transport.

One child was chasing a stray dog with a stick trying to hit it which made me cringe. I refused to comment unless he actually struck the animal. It was really bothering me so I asked an elderly woman next to me if she would say something to his mother about not torturing the little beige and white spotted stray reservation dog, but she said, "If that boy hitting that dog bothers you so much, ask him to stop." I did exactly that. I asked his assumed mother, "Is that your son hitting that stray dog?" She snarled with a raised voice, "It's his dog! He can hit it with a stick if he wants to. Why don't you mind your own business?" I had learned my first valuable lesson about life on "the rez": Let the tribal authorities and council deal with social ills, or what they deemed as social issues, requiring attention. Contracted employees or prospective ones, as was my case, had to do their jobs first and let the tribe deal with their own problems as they defined them. Those perceived problems did not always align with Anglo definitions of societal problems. I was embarrassed and relieved as the helicopter roared into sight, hovering over the green rapidly-moving leaves on the cottonwood trees that bordered the landing field.

Two weeks had gone by when I received a call from Mr. Argus, the school's incredibly-eccentric K-8 principal, a man who looked like he just jumped off the "Electric Company Greatest Episodes" DVD. He had wavy greased hair that fell a little below his droopy shoulders. He wore thick eyeglasses and his usual dress was in 70s-era bellbottom pantsuits that were too tight around the crotch area and had to have originated in a secondhand store in Somewhere, USA. Mr. Argus was what a male friend of mine would call "a weird duck." Mr. Argus asked if I had had time to think about the teaching position. He offered the following, "Hello. This is Principal Argus calling on behalf of the Havasupai Elementary School and Havasupai Tribal Council to extend an offer of employment from us to you. If you are serious about teaching in Supai, I suggest that you put your things in storage and arrive by August fifteenth for teacher orientation. The second grade teacher, Ms. Honeyuptewa, will be happy to share her duplex with you, which is attached to the BIA police headquarters." For those who have no idea, "BIA" stands for "Bureau of Indian Affairs." He gave me until the end of that week to give the tribe an answer either way.

He finished the conversation by saying that I was chosen unanimously by him and the tribal council which, he said, was highly unusual when an outsider was hired. He quickly mandated, "Let us know immediately what you decide." Then he hung up on me without a "goodbye." He was always rushed in his conversation and had bizarre body language akin to a poor mime's performance, where I could never figure out what he or she was gesturing. Even so, I was impressed by the children, their family members, and the tribal council. I remembered the warm reception that I had received from the tribe, the same warmth that has sustained their relationships with outsiders for centuries.

I liked the idea of living in an America where two of our country's largest social ills, alcohol abuse and guns, were illegal. The only negative of my interview weekend had been the rude mother episode in regard to the dog-hitting debacle. Another great reason to take the job would be to clear my head regarding Scott. Another great draw to the job for me was an escape from city life hundreds of miles away from the blazing hot desert. There would be no sirens, stop lights, or vehicle exhaust. *How did you say "Yes" in Supai?*

I took several days to make a decision. I would get an opportunity to be immersed in a culture that has survived thousands of years. I thought about the distance from the Phoenix area and all that I liked about modern life. *Could I live without all of the modern conveniences? How nice would no traffic be on my way to work?* My mind was made up. I would be the fourth and fifth grade combined classroom teacher at Havasupai Elementary School. I called my most recent love interest, Scott, to ask if I could store my things in part of his garage. I also asked if he minded getting my mail there because the Pony Express took several days longer than most American mail routes. The Pony Express was a romantic but slow institution, no matter how wonderful its longevity may be on its last route to and from the Havasupai Reservation. He agreed to temporary accommodations of my odds and ends. I would miss my friends and my almost-boyfriend, but the people of the blue-green water were pulling me down those eight miles of canyon trail into their alternate American existence.

Isolation from modern America sounded more appealing with each traffic jam, car horn, and inhaled exhaust cloud that I experienced while taking care of loose ends "up top." Excessive noise, traffic, and a disconnection from the natural world had never appealed to me. In a way, I see why many Native Americans and Amish Americans reject many aspects of modern life or modern ways of living. These cultures, for the most part, enjoy the peace, quiet solitude, and lack of modern interference with nature or one's cultural beliefs. The Havasupai tribe also knows that they do not need traffic, sirens, smog, or pavement to have a functioning society, albeit a small society with a population of approximately five hundred members. If anyone needed a fix of "modern America," he or she could go "up top" to get a taste of it on holidays, weekends or on school vacations.

I would be a tribal employee and resident of Supai, Arizona, and was committed to meeting my teaching goal of making sure that each of my students was proficient in their core subject areas at grade level. My commitment to maintaining the tribe's heritage and to include their native language was also unwavering. It was a multi-tasker's dream teaching position where I would have to quickly change roles from fourth to fifth grade teacher throughout the school day. I welcomed the teaching concept of what seemed to me like a one-room schoolhouse environment on the Havasupai Reservation. My adventurous spirit was fully engaged. To know Supai is to love it. It is a place that will lull anyone to a calmer, simpler time with nonstop country music on the general store's cash register-area radio. If any people understood those solitary, emotionally intense cowgirl and cowboy lyrics, it was the Havasupai. They were still living a rough and tumble western-style life. It was no spaghetti western. These folks were survivors of the real Wild West, even down to the wild horses that ran freely through the village center and reservation trails unexpectedly.

The attractive people and natural wonders piqued my curiosity. The tribe's high level of self-suffiency on the floor of the Grand Canyon was impressive and phenomenal. The opportunity to hopefully make a difference in the lives of my fourth and fifth graders was both exciting and a personal risk worth taking. Children are this country's future. All children in the United States are entitled to an effective public education guaranteed by the federal government. Being born in an isolated rural community should not prevent any American children from following their dreams and realizing their full potential as this country's caregivers. Although teaching in the Grand Canyon would be more difficult in terms of readily available resources, that was a challenge that I would willingly tackle for the tough, bright, and beautiful Havasupai children whose favorite activities were very unlike mainstream American children's leisure pleasures. Havasupai kids spent their spare time taming wild horses and whooping battle cries throughout the village at the top of their lungs. These children tended to domesticated creatures like goats, chickens, and mules. These kids swam in, and jumped off of, pristine waterfalls and waded in crystal turquoise creeks instead of an ocean or swimming pool.

Being completely enamored with the tribe was another reason for making such a major life change in their honor. It was a great sense of obligation I felt for these people that was inexplicable to family and friends. My feelings surpassed any simple explanation. The strong feelings of dedication to the tribe took me back to my first and final Reserve Officers Training Corps (ROTC) class when, as a college freshman, I had pondered going back into the active Army as an officer. I received a failing grade on my first warfare historical research project because I had written from the perspective of Chief Sitting Bull and his Oglala Sioux tribal members in the study of his effectiveness as a warrior and Custer's failure as an Army commander. My class professor and captain told me that in order to keep my grades above failing perhaps I should begin writing about successful Army commanders and combat missions.

To this day, I do not see why praise should be given to Custer, a genocidal egomaniac who killed all of his battalion's men, including himself, for his hatred of the Sioux tribe. His battle plan was foolish and resulted in one of the most shameful massacres in our nation's military history. My point to the ROTC commander was that even the best laid military battle plans can end in disaster if the commander underestimates his "enemy." Custer was an American failure and I felt he should be depicted as such. I cannot stand when bloodthirsty military American commanders from our nation's formative years are placed on a pedestal, especially someone like Custer. He had been on the edge of being thrown out of West

Point several times for his disrespectful and erratic behavior. He was no hero of westward expansion and I refused to paint him as such. I am well-read regarding the genocide that took place courtesy of our military in that time period. If Army bullets didn't work to decrease Native American numbers, the European diseases did. Some tribes were driven to extinction for all of the above reasons. A killer is a killer. A victim is a victim. Western expansion wasn't always pretty expanses of amber waves of grain. Lewis and Clark couldn't have made it without Sacagawea. With that said, let's move on to my own westward venture into Native American country in the name of education.

Mid-August came quickly that summer. Scott and his son expressed sadness at my departure, yet Scott still felt that he needed to shop around. I wished him luck with his quest. It was time for me to go down to the reservation and clear my head of all Scott-related drama. This woman's goals and ambitions would not wait for any man, not even one whom I loved so much. He needed to find out if he was more interested in marriage or playing the field. His first marriage had left him both bitter and jaded on the whole marriage concept. My new roommate was Dorothy Honeyuptewa a petite thin Hopi woman about a decade older than I am. Dorothy was obviously a hesitant participant in her roommate situation. She had not wanted to offer her spare bedroom to an "Anglo," she informed me one week after moving in. She said "Anglo" as a descriptive term for people like me a lot. She also made a lot of generalizations about non-Native American people injecting "All you Anglos" this or that into almost every conversation with me, which was irritating. Chris Rock would have had fun with Dorothy's eager bigotry. I had moved in with the Hopi female equivalent of Archie Bunker and it was really uncomfortable for me to have to bite my tongue. Ms. Honeyuptewa would behave rudely toward me with racial undertones such as not wanting me to drink out of any of her cups or eat off of her plates. I was expecting her to put red tape through the middle of the kitchen with Native- or Anglo-

Only sections. It seemed that I was taking one for the "Anglo"-American team. Dorothy was troubled and it wasn't just my DNA that she didn't care for.

It came to my attention that she and the married BIA police chief were lovers. She was a Hopi mistress who wanted her taboo relationship with the half-native chief kept a dirty little secret. She didn't want any Anglo eyes observing her immoral liaison as she walked next door for her sexual gratification. I wanted no part of it. Thank the Creator that a wild horse crossed my path one morning and then every morning for some granola and apples. He was my large, yellow-haired wild stallion friend with a messy mane and huge brown puppy dog eyes that told the story of his loneliness. He was a calm loyal horse that needed a friend as badly as I did.

It wasn't that I didn't care for Miss Honeyuptewa. She was simply set in her ways. Dorothy was not willing to have her sex life diminished by having a long-term guest, especially an "Anglo" one, in her territory. It was my hope that another teacher or tribal member had a room or house for rent. She apologized one evening by saying, "I know I have been hard on you but I was forced to let you stay in my spare room by Mr. Argus, not by choice." All of a sudden, I was part of her perceived "Anglo Invasion" and she was not a fan. Dorothy was happy that I was looking for another place to live. The one good thing about having Dorothy for a roommate was her explanations of different elements of her Navajo culture. Navajo people believe that nature is stronger than any person.

Dorothy's brother was a *kachina* artist for the Navajo tribe. Some of his work can be found at the Heard Museum in Phoenix, Arizona. Kachina's are an important symbol of Navajo culture and each has its own spirit and energy attached to it. She explained girls' advancement to adulthood through ceremonies that are part of the four day *Kinaalda* and the significance of the coiled "Princess Leia" hair of Navajo girls. She also told me the importance of dancing, music, and community involvement, as well as a Navajo girl's ability to hand crush corn to make into a Navajo cake called *alkaan* as another right of passage to womanhood. Her cultural insights were priceless to a young woman new to reservation life who had only read books about Navajo culture. A real tribal member is always a better source than a history book. Dorothy was living proof of that as a firsthand tribal member-cum-historian of the First Mesa Navajo nation. No "Anglo" could have told me about Navajo life better than Ms. Honeyuptewa had. Once I was out of her personal space, she and I became friendlier. I believe that the chief had filed for divorce, or so he told Dorothy. For her sake, I hoped the Chief was sincere. They made a cute couple aside from the impossibility of solidifying it publicly while I lived in Supai.

In Native American culture, it is taboo for a woman to cheat on a husband, but social suicide for a man to do so. The Havasupai tribe remains, for the most part, a matriarchal one, so men tend to follow the lead of their wives as well as female tribal elders and have issues if the opposite occurs. Some of the men had been kicked out of the tribe for committing adultery or other immoral, unsavory, anti-community acts such as sexual assault. While I lived there, the tribe was trying to get rid of a newly-convicted sex offender. He was not allowed to leave the confines of his property or to speak to any reservation women or children. I would see tribal men speaking to him briefly. When I walked by, most of the time he would stare out of his front door or windows. The tribe wanted him gone because he was bad for the tribe's people and image with the tourists. Every step was being taken to legally remove him from the reservation because his presence could affect tourism, and tourism pays the bills in Supai.

My teaching assistant was Kat. She taught me the basic history, customs, and culture of the tribe. She also taught me basic Supai words which would help me to better communicate with and discipline the children. She invited me to her home on several occasions for sugar-free treats and tea because she was type 2 diabetic. Kat was a big, beautiful woman with dark brown eyes and jet black hair that she usually wore in a ponytail. She was a member of one of the most powerful families in the Havasupai tribe. Her nephew was in our class and she would quickly keep him under control by threatening to tell his grandmother, who was his guardian, if he misbehaved. She often scolded one of my favorite, most challenging, ornery students, Ambrose, for committing un-American acts such as ripping all the "White Presidents" down off of the classroom wall before I arrived in the mornings because none were like him. She would also put the American flag back in the holder when he would fly off the handle about how his flag was the Havasupai flag, not the American flag. He would wave the flag angrily into the air like a sickened Native American rebel who did not think that the stars and stripes quite represented all American people. He would also choke himself to try to get a free high in my class which was very frowned upon by the tribe and me because of its oxygen-depriving effects on the choker. His mother worked full-time at the tribe's café and his stepfather ran mules in and out of the canyon to provide for their two sons. They worked hard to keep their sons out of trouble.

There was a new teacher in the village about three weeks into the school year. His name was Michael. He was a music teacher who had come from the Chandler school district near Phoenix. The Chandler administrators didn't like his "wild" hair, ripped jeans, or free-spirited attitude so they told him that he was on the short list. He was more about John Lennon and a lot less about John Philip Sousa as far as his musical leanings were concerned. He took himself off of the Chandler short list and went to work on the Havasupai reservation. Michael had taught, as I had, in poverty-stricken areas of Arizona, so he, too, was excited about teaching at a fully federally-funded school. He was a total character. He had a Music Education degree from Arizona State University and played acoustic guitar. His slightly-wavy hair was walnut with blond streaks and shoulder length, far from being anti-establishment. He looked French down to his dark olive tanned skin with a Sarkozy nose and thin frame. His personality was cheerful. He worked to boost the children's self-esteem, pride of heritage, and community-building through his musical selections. I will never forget when I overheard the second grade class sing "This Land is Your Land." What a beautiful sound emitting from the mouths of Native American babes. It was inspirational. Michael and I became good friends.

As in any small town in this country, rumors traveled quickly that Michael and I were an item. It was completely untrue. He was engaged to be married. Michael wanted his fiancée June to come down to the village to stay during the school year. She was a Christian missionary's daughter. When I first met her, June looked exotic with her brightly-colored African head scarf along with what looked like a colorful Peruvian patterned embroidered baby doll top, faded blue jeans, and leather sandals that had very sturdy soles. Michael and June were a perfect match. The two had purchased several acres of land in Williams, Arizona, for a bargain price of fifteen thousand dollars per acre. It was a multi-acre scrub brush and pinon pine-dotted land parcel with their RV and water tank on it and nothing more. It was a retreat for inseparable lovers who hoped to be married in the near future. Michael had bought June a gorgeous ring with the most fabulous shiny ruby on it, a more colorful option to the traditional diamond. They were both adamantly against the diamond trade. June had seen the dirty dealings of the diamond trade firsthand as a preacher's daughter in Africa. Forced servitude and deaths of innocent Africans related to the diamond trade were enough to sway her from ever buying an untraceable diamond.

June had been bombarded with fundamentalist Christianity most of her life and vowed that she would never be a part of any organized religion ever again, much to her reverend father's disappointment. She especially disliked Christian evangelical radio stations "selling right-wing propaganda via the radio waves" as she described their Christian "sales tactics." She and Michael enjoyed listening to Carol King, Pink Floyd, Bob Dylan, and many other classic rock and folk artists. We thought about the living arrangements. Michael was staying in a room at the tribal hotel. I was putting up with Dorothy's dislike of having me live with her. Dorothy wanted to live alone. June suggested that the three of us live together. Michael and I had hoped June would want to do this because it would save us a lot of money all the way around.

We all agreed that there would be safety in numbers. We teachers had to stick together. The three of us asked for a two-bedroom "brown house" rental. They are called "brown houses" because they were modeled after the brown wood-paneled forest ranger cabins, built more for function than for aesthetics. They look just like U.S. Forest Service cabins, although more upscale with a flushing toilet and modern amenities like washer and dryer hook-ups. There was no laundromat in Supai. The only drawback was the absence of both a clothes washer and dryer in our brown house. We would have to wash our dirty clothes by hand with old-fashioned laundry soap. Our bathtub would become the busiest area in our house between scrubbing ourselves and our filthy clothes. Our clothes usually had a thick coating of dirt so red that the stains took several washes to get out. Some of the red dirt stains never came out. I had to forgo wearing light-colored fabrics in Supai, Arizona. We used to get a chuckle or two from watching extravagantly-dressed city slicker tourists who wore a lot of white just like in one of the desert scenes from "The English Patient." We would watch and grin because we knew that in a matter of minutes those clothes would soon be ruined and permanently out of wardrobe circulation. I stocked my closet with dark pants, my favorite being the burgundy ones, and lots of dark-colored shirts, dresses, and socks to hide the Supai red soil blight.

I was happy to leave Dorothy's den to move in with my two newest friends. I fed my old wild horse friend some granola and an apple on my way out of the duplex, telling the beautiful blonde Indian horse that I would be a mile up the path if he wanted to find me. He was pale gold with a dirty blond mane. I was positive that he had energetically and courageously earned each one of the scars on his body. His eyes were tired and calm, as usual. He had kept me company in my down-time before Michael and June came to the village. He was my faithful unbroken mustang. I loved to see him in the peaceful, raven-caw-filled mornings. I enjoyed giving him food that he didn't have to fight or scavenge for. Now he would have to depend on Dorothy, who was unavailable to all but the married part-time Havasupai police chief. Putting my arms around his big sturdy neck, I kissed my wild blonde horse on his well-scarred muzzle. He just let out a grunty sigh. It was time to move into my own chosen space with June and Mike. It was an excellent arrangement for us. We were less lonely, shared food, cleaning, and utility costs. We were not big television fans and the hefty cost of buying a satellite dish was out of the question. Instead of TV, we would listen to the Navajo station or National Public Radio. There was a country music station, but no one liked it except me. I would listen to country music either at the tribe's general store or on the radio when my roommates were away from the house. We had records to play on Mike's turntable and speaker system. We would sing familiar songs while Mike played guitar. He and June were leaving Supai for the weekend. I would be at the house alone for the first time since I had moved in. The two would check on my car "up top" in the hilltop parking lot. They would call to let me know that they had made it out as soon as they arrived in the nearest town. It was strange being by myself for the first time in a long time.

They left every weekend that they could, so I would have co-workers or Agnes Champlain's son, our neighbor, check on me when my roommates were gone in the morning and at night to make sure that I didn't have any trouble. I was thankful for Alexander Graham Bell's invention of the telephone, my only mode of communication other than the Pony Express with which to communicate with the world "up top" and other non-Canyon inhabitants. I had a Maglight for protection and knew how to defend myself if I had to. I knew where to hit an attacker and I had good aim. I would lock the doors and windows nightly. Several of the tribe's women told me that if anything out of the ordinary happened that I could stay with them on the weekends. I had become part of the tight-knit community. Part of me thought, "*You have to be brave and show everyone that you aren't afraid of being alone on the reservation.*" The more sensible side thought, "*Go rent a horse and hightail it out of here before the heavy late-night drinking starts and late-night horse riders start lurking throughout Supai.*" Night brought a pitch black Supai, home of many wild animals, with a few wild animals of the human variety. Some tribal members drank prohibited liquor and, less frequently, used illicit drugs, with marijuana being the canyon drug of choice.

When a society gets rid of liquor, some people move on to a more dangerous high, as was sometimes the case in Supai. A few of the tribe's older teens always smelled like marijuana and were on mental absences when they should have been cleaned up and in school. The tribal council caved to the drug culture via a reggae concert funded by the tribe. For most of the people living in Supai, this concert was just clean fun. For some of the younger concert goers, it most likely seemed like permission to use marijuana at will. The music was excellent; however, it unintendedly caused heightened interest in marijuana as an escape for the tribe's young men and women. Some of the teenagers who were indulging in marijuana looked terrible and had drugged, lost expressions on their faces. Bob Marley was seen as some kind of tribal savior to the young Native Americans. *How had these teenagers gotten turned on to this lifestyle? Why was the tribe bending its principals to please a small fraction of its membership?* It then dawned on me that this was probably the only way that the tribe's adolescents could rebel. Their rebellion led them to listen to reggae, skip the medicine man, as well as the ancient traditional ritual sweat lodge, and opt for some stronger illegal medicine.

While I listened to the music with my students and their families, several of the children urged me to dance. Who could pass up a great reggae beat with one's students and parents? It was an honor to have my students' acceptance just a month into the school year. I danced with my co-workers as well. We education adventurers knew good music when we heard it. We also knew that the Havasupai elders mostly thought of this event as a community-building activity, as well as a way for tribal members to give to a good cause: themselves. I think dancing that night and being in attendance earned me some much sought-after respect and friendship with the tribe's families. No one can be an effective teacher without having a strong relationship with the community that he or she teaches in.

My first weekend alone in Supai had gone better than expected. I had only one smashed older male Havasupai scoundrel race back and forth on the trail that was to one side of our home. As I looked out the front door, he and I looked at each other. He and his horse came to an abrupt stop. His horse whinnied and reared. The Champlain's son's porch lights came on. The man looked toward me, shakily pointing his index finger at me and yelled, "Teach me, teacher! What can you teach me? I'm an old juvenile, teacher. A juveniiiiile!" Wherever he had formed his views on educators, I had had no personal part in it. Being a fourth-generation immigrant, none of my ancestors had ever owned slaves, nor had they harmed Native Americans. I quickly shut my front storm door, double locked it, and decided to put my foam Army surplus store ear plugs in to get his ranting out of my already overstimulated ears.

October began as the weather suddenly became much cooler. It was time to put the sandals and short sleeves away until spring. My teaching assignment was going well. We had a meeting in the school's multipurpose room where an education representative from the Bill and Melinda Gates Foundation was informing us of the arrival of the Internet to the Havasupai Elementary School, Tribal administrative buildings, and the community center. Everyone, especially the children, was noticeably excited. Bill and Melinda Gates were donating all of the computer equipment and a satellite associated with bringing the Internet and computer technology to the Havasupai

Tribe. The only cost to the tribe would be a minimal monthly fee for satellite service, not bad considering that the satellite would provide Internet access to the five hundred plus-or-minus Havasupai reservation residents for the first time ever. We would all be getting in-depth news coverage as it happened at CNN.com and other websites. No longer would we get our daily news in short bursts on the radio or two days late via the Pony Express. The teaching staff could now create lessons that tied in with live events or information on-line. I eagerly anticipated the computers and equipment designated for the school's new computer room.

On the Friday that the satellite and computer equipment came to Supai, everyone in the village gathered at the Community Center to see history in the making. A very handsome, young burly Supai man with an alluring smile and equally alluring large almond-shaped, dark brown eyes was leading a mule with pieces of the satellite dish hanging from the saddle and straddling the light gray pack mule's backside. This man was one of the regular pack horse and mule operators who watched the tourists and others "up top" to see who needed a mule or horse. Even the mule seemed to be smiling in that nostalgic moment as the Havasupai moved abruptly from the twentieth century into the twenty-first via pack mule. I found myself unable to stop smiling as the tall, dark, and very handsome young Havasupai ham smiled proudly and almost professionally for the press photographers and the Gates Foundation videographer who caught the moment on film and in photos for the rest of the world, the Gateses, and their foundation members to see. Fletcher was the young heart-accelerating Havasupai man's name. After the satellite mule was grabbed by one of his co-workers, he walked up to me. He asked if I enjoyed teaching at the school. I cheerfully reported, "So far, so good. How's the hauling business treating you?" I was thinking about how he had missed his calling as a television or movie star. He answered, "It has to be good, because I have a little boy to care for." I was intrigued.

*Had I just met the Havasupai version of my quasi-boyfriend?* He was single, well-adjusted, and flirting with me in plain view of the entire tribe, including his family members. He was undoubtedly brave and extremely sexy. My interest was up for this reserved and, at times, showy Native American man. I was prepared to get to know this intelligent, friendly, hard-working man better. Fletcher asked if he could stop by the house after dark to attempt to pre-empt the highly active Supai rumor mill. I invited him to come over after the sun disapeared behind the walls of the canyon around 7:00 o'clock. The extra time would give me a few hours to primp for our "secret" rendezvous. Fletcher showed up promptly at seven o'clock. I saw a gorgeous smiling face through my front door window. The sight of his smile made my blood pump faster. There standing so confidently and tall was Fletcher, the blazing hot object of my infatuation. He wasted no time coming in and taking a seat in the modest kitchen which he told me was "nice." Mike and June were out hiking after dark to give me time to myself. Fletcher did not waste time as he confessed his feelings to me, "I've liked you ever since I saw how much your students like you at the school. They talk about how much you make them laugh and how you make them do too much homework. You're also real pretty. Whenever you walk by me and my pack horse work buddies, I just want to stop working and get to know the smart sexy new teacher better."

I didn't know what to say. The same pull that he felt toward me was what I felt for him. There was a lusty, powerful feeling overtaking me. He grabbed my face so gently and so suddenly in his big strong hands that butterflies took flight within me. He said, "I think of you all the time. I want to get to know you. The mother of my child, Nicole, will be very jealous if she finds out that we've been spending time together. She is harmless. There is no future for her and me. My son is my only concern. It didn't end well with her. I will not marry a woman that I don't love, no matter what my family says."

At least he didn't care to enter into a pointless marriage based on the creation of a child. I still do not understand why people do that. The children can see the absence of love. It makes kids feel insecure and unstable when they live in a miserable household. The effect of bad marriages on children has been researched in-depth and there can be negative long term effects on a child's self-esteem. Fletcher was correct not to enter a loveless marriage, but he was also wrong to get himself into that situation to begin with. That said, he was a doting, loving father to his son who was clever and high-spirited like his father.

We were deep in conversation when we saw my roommates stepping up to the front deck stairs. Fletcher took his warm hands from my hand and face to quickly straighten up. His cover was about to be blown. He had the "kid caught with his hands in the cookie jar" look. That was when I started to laugh a belly laugh and couldn't stop. We had just had the most serious conversation and had to change characters quicker than a student in a method acting workshop. Fletcher stood up like a soldier at attention as Christian walked in after June. I could imagine him barking, "Sir, yes, sir!" to Mike, who had become like a brother to me since we began teaching together. My laughter left me and I regained my composure as my roommates made their entrance. Fletcher was now a humble guest, hoping for a positive greeting which was exactly what he received. Mike had a huge Cheshire cat grin on his face. He could barely contain himself. He advised us, "Have fun you two. Remember to come up for air and watch for village gossips." Then, Fletcher and I laughed so hard that we both had tears in our eyes and our sides hurt. Fletcher suggested that we sit on the deck chairs outside and look at the stars.

He knew all of the standard constellations as well as some Native American ones that I enjoyed learning about immensely, especially the rain-making stars which are supposed to predict when a storm was approaching. He kept me warm with his thick, long arm around my shoulders and he laid his jacket over my upper body. He was a gentleman. It had gotten so late that we were well into Saturday already. Our date had to come to an end, but before it did Fletcher slowly moved in for a goodnight kiss that warmed me top to bottom. That kiss was like a bonfire on a cold autumn night. It was one of the sweetest goodnight kisses of my life. His kisses were as sensuous as I had imagined them to be. He asked if he could see me the following evening and I happily obliged. We didn't know where our new involvement was going, but we were both willing to find out. Both of us were in need of companionship and a little bit of romance, two things that he and I were deprived of. Sleep came easily that night after my romantic interlude with Fletcher, whose smiling face and irresistible lips I couldn't get out of my mind. I hoped that our intimate moments together would find their way to my dreams that night.

I was as giddy as a schoolgirl the following day. I passed Fletcher on my hike to the falls to find some peace and solitude. It was November and the air was consistently chilled. I missed swimming in the centrifuge of the blue-green water of the Havasu Falls. My vertigo kept me from ascending the primitive ladder in the rock cliff down to the bottom of the steep Mooney Falls. Mooney Falls was named for a pioneer who had once lived in Supai and fell to his death from the top of the falls. Navajo Falls got its name similarly except the Navajo scout had been found murdered at the bottom of the falls in the pool there. Swimming at the Navajo and Havasu Falls was exotic because it resembled a tropical location without the palm or coconut trees. The tan soil surrounding the pool at the Havasu Falls is strange to see because of the red rock seen all along the walls of the Grand Canyon as well as its trails.

The bottom of the canyon between its walls looked like a beach alongside an ocean. It all made sense to me that ancient seas once ran through what is now the Grand Canyon over one hundred million years ago. I found ancient brachiopod fossils in a chunk of limestone while hiking the canyon trail into Supai immediately after a period of local flooding. A Havasupai postman told me to keep the fossils and teach my students about them, which I did. He told me to keep my eyes looking downward to find fossils or ancient artifacts. I thanked him for the helpful hint. I then asked him which sections of the trail were the worst due to the recent flooding. He happily advised me on the rough spots. I only had a short amount of time left to get all the way down to the village before dark.

During the last leg of the hike into Supai, about two miles from the village center, were flood warning signs. I noticed some strange dark colored rocks bunched together along the canyon wall under some trees. I picked through them with my hands and felt something sharp. *What was that?* I wondered what I would uncover in the pile of rocks and sand. I noticed a jagged knife blade or spearhead in my hand. The charcoal-colored stone looked like a flint tool from a prehistoric era. The Havasupai elders had told me that a civilization had lived there many thousands of years before them but had vanished. Was this one of their spearheads or knife blades? The exquisite nature of this small piece, which was still stained by blood from its years of usefulness during the Stone Age, was further proof of ancient civilizations at the Grand Canyon. I was impressed by its jagged edge and sharpness. The indentations looked like my butcher knife at home. It could probably still be used as a cutting tool. I kept it for research and teaching purposes. I found out years later in a geology class that it was likely a spearhead used as an animal skinning instrument, thus the blood stains were only on one side of the blade. Its sharp tip could be used to kill an animal when it was tied to a wooden spear.

I had a long hike ahead of me and the sun was disappearing behind the western wall of the canyon. The days in the canyon are shorter than anywhere else in the continental United States because of the very high walls keeping the sun's rays out, with the exception of during midday. I savored the daylight because it left by mid-afternoon or early evening, depending upon whether it was fall or winter. Even so, those uninterrupted starry skies were some of the clearest that I have ever seen. The higher elevation made me feel like I could touch the stars if I reached high enough. The Grand

Canyon over Supai was a no-fly zone for any commercial aircraft other than helicopters in or out of the village. I never saw exhaust plumes or flashing lights, or had to experience any annoying air traffic noise. The only sounds at night were from little tree frogs and grasshoppers that resembled locusts, who were awaiting their winter departures. I liked the melody of the creatures that played every night like a dependable cover band. The only time that the creatures were very quiet was during rainfall or a thunderstorm. When it rains in the canyon, water pours over into it like an overflowing bathtub in reverse. Rainbows would form not only in the spray of the thundering waterfalls, but at the sides of the canyon during sun-streaked rain showers.

Fletcher visited me on Sunday nights for a month or so, until we both decided that we would make better friends than a couple. His heart was unavailable to anyone. My heart was still aching from being so far away from Scott. It was a bittersweet ending, because I would miss those warm dark caramel kisses at dusk as I waited for my roommates to show up. Fletcher's sister was the tribe's Head Start director, a class act who was very glamorous. She was always wearing the latest fashions and near-perfect make-up. She was a feminist Indian princess, constantly doing all that she could to generate more funding for the preschool and its programs. I admired her as much as I did Agnes Champlain for making the reservation a better place to live, even if they had to swallow some pride to get help. She had classy grit and made unapologetic efforts to make the reservation a better place for Havasupai women to work and to raise their children.

One weekend, I decided to go "up top" to the town of Seligman on Historic Route 66. Fletcher's sister needed a ride to the Flagstaff airport. Although it was out of the way, she was Fletcher's sister and so I would help her to get to Phoenix. She either had no idea that her brother and I had been dating for some time or she was a great actress. As we drove away from the Hualapai Hilltop down BIA route 18 to Route 66, she expressed how she wished Fletcher would marry Nicole, his son's mother. I told her not to hold her breath, because rumor had it that he was not in love with her. I added that I had heard that Nicole had planned the supposed "unplanned pregnancy" in an attempt to take him off the market. She seemed disillusioned and a bit miffed by my apparent insider's knowledge. Part of me wanted to say, "I know Fletcher isn't in love with that woman because he started to fall for me, but wasn't ready for a serious relationship. He's definitely not going to go after that snake Nicole!" Instead, I calmly said, "Your brother is busy being a great father. That is obvious. You cannot create feelings for someone that never existed to begin with. One thinks 'fling.' The other thinks 'forever.' Fletcher seems to me like a free spirit." She smiled and said, "Maybe he'll meet a nice woman like you who will straighten him out." Straightening a man out did not sound like anything that I wanted to build my life around. I preferred self-starters.

After dropping Fletcher's sister off at the airport, I headed west on Route 66 to the funky little Historic Route 66 Motel in Seligman, Arizona. I requested Room 111, where Will Rogers was rumored to have slept. After checking into the motel, I walked over to the Road Kill Café, where I had two very tall light beers and one of the biggest and most flavorful one hundred percent Angus beef cheeseburgers and seasoned fries that I have ever eaten. They had an excellent juke box there, lots of memorabilia, and fun names on the menu that referenced squashed animals along the Route 66 that you may have passed on the way to the café, such as "swirl of squirrel." The ridiculous menu names would put a smile on my face and the motto of "You kill it and we'll grill it" was so absurd that it was worth a laugh. After getting my fill and mingling with the locals and tourists, I headed back to my room for a comfortable night's sleep. There was a homey German-style restaurant called West Lilo's Café across from the motel. The omelets menu was out of this world for a one-horse-and-a-few-prairie-dogs town. The coffee was definitely worthy of being called German-strength. For lunch later on that day, after checking out all of the local shops, I got a hot dog and root beer float at the A&W stand a few paces away from West Side Lilo's, where the gas station was. After I got my blood pumping again, it was time to fill the gas tank and head back to the reservation. I looked down at my watch and saw that it was almost three o'clock in the afternoon. The helicopter landing at Hualapai Hilltop was over an hour away from the gas station following the speed limits. It became dark at about 4:30 p.m., due to the shorter November days. I drove as quickly and safely as possible up Route 66 and BIA Route 18 to get to the Havasupai trailhead at the hilltop on time. I passed and weaved through deer, tribal horses, and the tribe's free-ranging cattle that would nonchalantly venture in front of my little sports coupe. Luckily, there was no ice or snow on the roads, so the sharp turns were easy to navigate, providing that there were no distracted random tourist drivers swerving on the unfamiliar road.

Besides young teenagers, the huge Cadillacs with a speeding elderly person at the helm scared me the most. When seniors were speeding, their reflexes could be too slow for BIA Route 18 where, at points, there was no guard rail, just a lot of trees if you weren't paying attention or trying to avoid hitting an object or creature feature. The one lane road could be treacherous and could momentarily turn you into a stunt driver. I had never gone off the road due to another person's driving, however I did swerve a few times during the frequent winter snowstorms at the hilltop elevation at the canyon's rim.

As I approached the final S curve to hilltop, I saw tourists from the last helicopter out leaving in the opposite direction that I was traveling in. As I entered the parking lot, it appeared that there were just a bunch of empty vehicles and two Havasupai men with eight horses and pack mules. They had just dropped off their last batch of tourists and were getting ready to board their horses "up top" for the night. I didn't have enough cash on me to rent a horse. What I did have was food and a little cash in exchange for one, so

I approached the men about my predicament. The last thing that I wanted to do was to hike to Supai in the freezing temperatures and early winter darkness of the mostly deserted canyon trail. Years earlier, I had learned how to ride Western style, so I explained to the horse owners that I knew how to ride. The Havasupai man who was the obvious businessman of the two, and a kind one, said, "You are my stepson Ambrose's teacher aren't you?" I answered affirmatively. He continued, "Looks like you missed the chopper and need a horse, or need to ask the sun to stay out for you an hour or two longer today.' Then he laughed a high pitched look-at-the-Anglo-without-a-ride sarcastic cackle while he held his sides. It was a pretty ridiculous situation, so I laughed at myself, too. Then, I asked, so embarrassed at my predicament and probably more shades of red than an apple orchard, "Can I please pay you to ride one of your horses down to the village?" He said, "I'll take payment in cash. It's fifty dollars for tourists, but for you, teacher, I'll be happy with twenty. Next time you run late make sure you have either a case of beer or soda with you and any of these guys will give you a horse. Just make sure the horse is broken-in because some of these guys are sadistic and like to see tourists or others go for a wild ride." Then he laughed hard all over again. I was a little taken aback by his last comment.

Was I going to get a "wild" pack horse or a calm one that would get me safely down to Supai? I wasn't in the mood for a wild ride through the sharp-cornered zigzag switchback trail or the steep rock stairs mid-trail on a trick pony. It wasn't an ideal situation and my funds were low, so I gave the well-humored gent my twenty dollars and a case of Coca-Cola. *There would be no soda this week except from the general store at double the price,* I thought to myself. My new friend saddled up the horse. She was very sturdy with dark chocolate brown fur and an almost-black streaked dark brown mane. She looked tired. He told me in parting, "This old girl will do. She has been down and back and up again, so she may be a little cranky," then he laughed along with his business partner, followed by well wishes from the gleeful onlookers. Perhaps it was my outfit that they thought was so funny. I had on a pair of Columbia hiking pants, a thick sweatshirt, and a Polarfleece jacket. It wasn't cold that day, but it never hurt to be prepared for whatever might come next.

It was sixty degrees Fahrenheit, which was practically a heat wave by Grand Canyon standards. My new waterproof cushioned hiking boots were perfect for about any outdoor activity. The horse's owner, Ambrose's step-dad, helped me with my backpack and belongings by lending me two big saddlebags. The two men carefully balanced and secured my belongings. They advised me to keep an even pace, "Slow and steady," they repeated over and over again as I took off. As I peered over the deep drop-off of the parking lot, I became petrified with fear. My horse clumsily headed straight for the first steep rock ledge step of the cliffside switchback. The distance down the side of the cliff looked like an abyss from atop my mare transportation assistant. I almost had to close my eyes as she descended those first railroad-tie-marked steep steps down the rapid descent off of the parking lot area. She was grunting her discontent at an already long day with plenty of miles logged. I patted her neck and head to let her know that I, too, was tired, in an attempt to help calm her down for the approximately nine miles that lay before us. All of a sudden, out popped a couple with three older children in front of my horse. I pulled back on her reigns softly ordering, "Whoa, girl." She completely ignored me and the human obstacles to her awaiting food and stall by clippety-clopping directly at them. The father practically rock climbed up the rocky hillside while the mother and the children quickly scattered to the far side of the trail away from my aggressive worn-out mare. The word "nag" was acquiring double meaning as I smiled and sheepishly stated, "I'm so sorry. This is a new horse and she obviously has her own mind. Please excuse us." Then I kept repeating that refrain for my tired old nag who was spent on all of humanity, especially tourists as was the case. Once we navigated through the ascending switchback hikers, on the last steep step edge, she walked so far over, that she was tipping toward the huge drop off of the trail when she regained her footing and began galloping faster toward the bottom of the canyon. I kept pulling her reigns. She kept ignoring me. Suddenly, we stopped so fast that the forward momentum of my body forced me to grab the saddle horn to prevent it from being lodged in my stomach. *What was this horse's problem, aside from complete canyon burnout?*

    She leaned her head down to have a snack of wild grasses and any other foliage that were in the vicinity of her mouth. The old girl was famished and I would have to wait until she was good and ready to move. She apparently didn't respond to flailing the reigns against her bowed neck. I decided to let her eat for about ten minutes then clicked my heels on her hips once and said, "Come on girl, giddy up!" She gave me a sideward glance that pretty much let me know that this was her show. The show would go on when she decided it would. I was just along for the ride. She was riding her way or not at all. By the time we reached the third cottonwood tree where she took an extended horse-y break, I lost my patience. It was beginning to get dark and we hadn't even gotten to the wet Havasu Creek rock ledge at the halfway point near the creek crossing.

    That's when I decided to dig my heels into her backside to get her attention and flailed the reigns hard. The old nibbler whinnied, stood straight up on her hind legs like a rodeo rebel in a roping contest and tried to shake me and my gear off her back. I held on for dear life, keeping my feet in the stirrups and grabbing her mane until I could firmly hold onto the saddle horn again. She just clunked her front hooves down defiantly while I tied her to a tree, jumped down, careful not to get dropkicked, and picked up my scattered goods. I would never be able to balance it the way my native friends had, so I threw it all in the saddlebags haphazardly

    It was like the horse's possessor had warned earlier. The sun wasn't waiting for me or Ms. Tired Hooves to get it together. Now

I was probably as irritated as she was, so we were evenly matched. She wanted off this trail ride as badly as I did so she upped the ante and sprinted for awhile. We made it to the slippery "halfway" rock steps. I slowed her down to a crawl to ascend the slippery creekside rocks because if we slid, we could both get badly hurt. This would not end like some bad spaghetti western with me shooting my old broken-legged horse with a cap gun. She and I were strong and ticked off. It was magical. We didn't slip and we both calmed down. We were approaching the two mile marker, which tickled me because I could see the first star of the evening above us. You can guess what I wished for.

The mature older mare clip-clopped almost leisurely as we neared the village. I could hear horses that were racing quickly behind us on the sandy well-traveled path. I thought to myself, *These had better be "friendlies" or they are going to have to deal with the two meanest broads in the canyon.* We were ready for anything. I took my police issue Maglight out to ward off any potential attack. My horse steered clear of them. My eyes tried to focus on the passersby in the dark canyon. It was Ambrose's older brother, with the rental provider of the fine steed that I rode upon. Ambrose's stepfather offered to lead the way to the village with his son. I appreciated their continued kindness. This last week of November would be the most challenging for me. The beginning of the month had been satisfying. My students, their families, and I were securely familiar with one another. Veteran's Day was wonderful and humbling when I was given recognition as an Army veteran with the gift of a Native American print heavy wool blanket, which the tribal council president wrapped around my shoulders during the ceremony. The tribe asked me to participate in their veterans' dance, which was a part of their culture before recorded history. It was a ceremony that was steeped in rich Native American history. It was an honor for this female veteran to be in the company of such brave Native American warriors.

Afterward there was dancing and games, such as the corn kernel game which baffles young and old alike because dried corn kernels are hidden in mounds of soil in such a way that you have to pretty much take a gamble on which mound they are hidden in. If you guessed correctly the first time, you would get a prize. There were no prizes for runners up, but plenty of chances were given to those who kept playing the game. We feasted on newly-hunted venison, kettle corn, freshly-grown vegetables, and peach desserts made with the peaches from Peach Springs, Arizona, which was near Kingman, and was the home of the Hualapai tribe. Peach Springs was once home to the kindergarten-through-twelve boarding school that was now abandoned. There was a peach festival each year to use up the peaches grown there. The hunters were sharing their deer hunting adventures with me, as well as their soldier stories, as we sat together to eat. I could not have dreamed up a better Veteran's Day. My father, a Vietnam Vet, would have liked the celebration, as he also enjoys deer hunting and shares the Native American love for country.

A favorite veteran of mine in the Havasupai tribe was an elderly Korean War vet who sat most of the time on a bench in front of the general store and post office building. He kept a close eye on everyone, especially the adolescents because, as he put it, "The young people are getting lazy and losing pride in their heritage." He was trying to work with the tribal council to get the teenagers more focused on school, so they would be able to serve the tribe and their country. His insights into the struggles of the tribe's young people were valuable to me as a new resident and teacher. He was noble to take on the social problems of the tribe and fight to get rid of them. His new battle was against social and cultural decay within his people, the enemy was within some of his fellow tribal members. The drugs, alcohol, and disrespect had to be eliminated from Supai life and he was leading the fight. I admired his knowledge, strong spirit, and honesty. He also had a biting sense of humor which was a necessity in small town life. We always called each other "soldier." He would say, "Huah!" which is the Army shout out. I would return his farewell with a

"Semper Fi!" for his being a Marine Corps veteran. I usually gave the Korea Marine veteran with the wooden cane and religiously worn dark blue cap a hug.

The work week began like every week before, comparing stories about our adventures "up top" or on the rez over the weekend. As my friend Lenora, the school's librarian, and I caught up with each other, a female junior high student appeared to be combative with her classmate who she was pushing away with force. This wasn't good. The other girl screamed, "Stop pushing me T." Then "T" (short for Terri) slapped her classmate across the face. I was horrified at what might happen next. *Why is this girl being so violent to her classmate?*

I immediately approached the young lady, asking her to come with me to the principal's office. She responded by saying, "Make me, b****." Dragging the derogatory word out for a spell, and then quickly slapped me across the face. I was outraged at this unpredictable assault. I proceeded to restrain the girl by using a walking type of restraint to get her to the principal's office. She clawed me the entire way. It was borderline unbearable. This had never happened to me outside of a mental health environment. Once we got to the principal's office, I explained that the young lady had temporarily lost her self-control, striking a classmate and then me. Mr. Argus told me, "This student is a he not a she, so let's clear that up." *Oh no! I was getting a transgender youth suspended.*

Although I knew his behavior was inexcusable, I felt a pang of empathy for his frustration with his gender identity and how that was most likely the cause of his aggressiveness. This poor child was being non-traditional in a place that embraced bravado, masculinity, and only allowed face paint for tribal ceremonies. Terri wanted make-up every day and not your war paint, smudge stick, or clay mound variety. I apologized for my ignorance of his pre-existing transgender situation and personal struggle for acceptance. He still deserved to do the time for his aggressiveness. He was given a three-day suspension. The principal then told me to never bring a tribal council member's child to his office again or he would fire me. I was unaware of the young man's lineage, only that I was fully aware of his aggressiveness toward female students and staff that should not be tolerated. My decision was to break up the fights and let his teacher deal with the repercussions, especially with the heavy tribal power behind his bad behavior.

The tribe was denying counseling for this boy's gender identity issues. This was a solid case of the tribe saying, "We do not accept this child's behavior and will not help him figure himself out." Homosexuality was a taboo subject among tribal members. There was little understanding of it and the consequences of homophobia were that Terri's outward demeanor and inner battle made him dislike himself and some in his community. Mainstream American struggles had a place in Supai, only there were not as many citizens who would publicly acknowledge certain diversity issues. I gave Terri as much support as possible, after the suspension, to let him know that I did not harbor any ill feelings toward him. I told him that if he ever needed someone to talk to that I was available during lunch hour or after school when an audience of his peers could not taunt him.

The weekend came quickly. It was a three-day Thanksgiving weekend for the reservation. Scott called asking if I would like to have dinner with his family at his parents' house in Chandler, Arizona. I told him that I was happy to go to their house for Thanksgiving dinner, but had to immediately return to Supai. We were excited about seeing each other for the holiday. I had missed him so much. I was relieved to be spending the holiday with him and his family. I told him that I would not get there until Saturday. On Friday, at about noontime, there was a knock on the door. It was a few of my students. They said out of order and out of breath, "Teacher, teacher. There's some man and little boy looking for you. Should we get them and bring them to you?" I told them to go get them and thanked them for being so thoughtful.

Scott and his son had come to bring me back to Chandler for Thanksgiving with his family. I didn't understand why he had brought his son, when I knew he had support in that arena. It is difficult getting reacquainted with an audience. It looked like the handiwork of a jealous ex-wife trying once again to throw a wrench in Scott's plans. The hike down the canyon was for children twelve years and older, not for a ten-year-old with limited hiking experience. But it made me happy that Scott had shown up. He and his son had hiked nearly ten miles to see me. Had Scott made up his mind to get serious, or was he just lonely? Fletcher had heard from his friends that I had male company so he came over right away. I thought to myself, *Oh no! How is this going to play itself out?* Fletcher was polite as he walked up to Scott and said, "Hello. You must be Scott. Nice to meet you." Fletcher looked at Scott's son Devin and said, "I have one of those, too," and shook Scott's and Devin's hands. Fletcher added, "Lara's a good woman. You'd better be good to her or you'll have to deal with me." He smiled as his thumb poked his chest about where his heart beat underneath.

Scott looked a bit puzzled and realized immediately that I had had companionship while in Supai. I had not played the damsel-in-waiting role of the romantically-needy woman who anxiously waited for him to return to me wholeheartedly. Life is too short to waste by awaiting a marriage proposal from a commitment-phobe. Scott looked a bit deflated, ego-wise, shook Fletcher's hand and said, "I know what a good person Lara is or I wouldn't be here." Fletcher nodded his head. Fletch gave me a hug and smiled at me as he walked away toward the village center. His quiet sophistication and sentimentality were what had led to such a satisfying brief liaison. He had a huge heart and was a good listener. Scott was determined to regain lost ground with me. I felt the same way toward him. I loved Scott and was impressed by his effort to see me on my level. His son was quite the adventurer. Devin was disappointed because he had not seen any animals on the trail with the exception of a desert squirrel. Thinking of the Road Kill Café menu item made me grin. We had an excellent meal that afternoon before catching the helicopter out of the canyon for Thanksgiving.

June was an excellent cook and had made a scrumptious Thai dish that could put hair on your chest. Scott and Devin slept on sofas in the living room.

Scott, Devin, and I headed for the field across from the community center where the helicopter was set to pick us up momentarily. One male tribal member walked by the outdoor seating area of the café, looked at Scott and loudly uttered, "Hygewi!" which is pronounced *Hi-gewey*. This is the worst racial epithet toward an Anglo in the Supai language. I didn't know the person who said it and Scott was wondering what he had said. I explained, "Sometimes being an anonymous tourist is easier here. Some people in the tribe might see you and think that you are going to take me away from my duties to the school children. Supai is a tight-knit community. They do not all like outsiders coming in to stir things up." Scott just shook his head replying, "I suppose it could have been worse." Scott didn't get worked up about it. He grew up among the Sioux tribe in South Dakota as a child growing up in Sioux Falls.

I told Scott a story about an incident at the beginning of the school year. I would sit outside of the school to finish my lunch. A repairman for the tribe would stop by to ask me how things are going. He would fill me in on the latest village talk around town. I would fill him in on all of the school's latest.

On one September Friday afternoon, I waited for the helicopter so I could get out of the canyon for a weekend for a stay at the Canyon Lodge in Seligman. An angry-looking native woman with a frown on her face looked in my direction as she walked straight toward me. She began speaking in a loud voice, "Teacher lady! Yeah, you! Stay away from my husband. I know you and him got something going on. You better just stay away from him!" This woman was so angry and, frankly, had me confused as to which Havasupai man she was referring to. I calmly asked, "Who is your husband, ma'am, because I have no idea who you are talking about?" She told me the repairman's first name. I defended myself with the following: "You have no reason to be concerned. We talk outside the school in plain view of others a few times per week about our jobs and nothing else. I am sorry if you don't trust your husband, but I can assure you that I'm not interested in him in a romantic way." Then I walked away from her confrontational jibberish.

I then had some inkling of how life must have been for women back in the Puritan days of early America. I felt like I had just received the Supai equivalent of the "Scarlet Letter S" for socializing with a Havasupai man who happened to be "M," for married. Luckily, we did not live in that era, or I would be shunned for being wrongfully-accused by a woman pointing, yelling, "Adulterer! Adulterer! She is stealing my husband! Get her! Punish her! Adulterer!" Other Supai women comforted me by saying, "Don't worry about her. She doesn't like him talking to any unmarried women. Older Supai women don't like younger women talking to their husbands. It is seen as disrespect. We know it's not true. She represents old superstitions about marriage. She's just trying to intimidate you," and the onlookers lost interest in the spectacle. I couldn't wait to get into the helicopter and to my hotel room at the Canyon Lodge. A nice couple from Nepal ran the small hotel. Each morning, they made fresh pastries and coffee for their guests. They knew me and would give me extra towels without me having to ask for them. They had a beautiful family. It was the last hotel on the road before heading to Kingman from Seligman. I wonder if they are still there. Once in the privacy of my room, I experienced a few hot teardrops of anger in reaction to the ugly public accusations and humiliation at the helicopter landing. I let the tears roll for a few short minutes and then stopped. I resolved to stay strong and not let cultural differences stand in the way of my teaching or making friends within the tribe. My positive attitude would not be shaken so easily by this cruel undeserved maltreatment.

Scott listened to my stories of the first two months of living in Supai. After a long drive to Chandler where Scott's parents were hosting Thanksgiving Dinner, I received a warm "welcome back" from Scott's family. It was like old times. Scott's brother and I had always had intense political conversations and Al Gore had just lost the Presidential election, so we were in an uproar over alleged vote tampering in Ohio and Florida. Everyone wanted to know about reservation life.

I explained that the Havasupai reservation was a complex tribal community with beautiful natural resources that attract many tourists from all over the world, a natural paradise at the bottom of the Grand Canyon. The Apaches had the luxury resort of Phantom Ranch, but they didn't have the falls and quiet tree-filled trails that Supai did. Supai wasn't a tourist gimmick and wasn't for those who expected to be pampered constantly. It was one of the only places in the United States where a person could stay on a Native American reservation and be immersed in a different culture. Supai was one of the best natural and cultural gems found in the United States. The only major barrier to village tourism was transportation. The three H's formula for transportation into or out of Supai was "X equals Horse, Helicopter, or Hike." If you wanted to meet some descendants of our nation's first inhabitants, you had to make an effort. We can all learn something from Native American culture and history. We would all do well to reach out to the founding fathers and mothers of our continent.

Scott and I hiked back to Supai the day after Thanksgiving. It was nice to get some alone time with him. It was a sunny late November day. Although chilly, we were in Polarfleece jackets with thick sweatpants and were also wearing warm hiking boots. We took an ample number of breaks on the natural rock ledges. We passed a burning horse that must have died on the trail. The Supai believe that the dead horse's spirit is released by burning it. I grabbed an old horse shoe that I had found not far from the burning animal. I hated the awful stench of burning horse flesh. It made me sad for the animal having to have a public cremation. It was not one the Supai's kinder traditions. It was a cool overcast day. Feeling comfortably primitive, we enjoyed an intimate nap wrapped in a thin Polarfleece blanket and not much else in a cave-like horizontal groove in the canyon wall. Scott's body against mine felt like thunder shaking the canyon walls. It was a powerful erotic intermission from hiking. He was so handsome with his dark tan, platinum blond tousled short hair, Statue of David physique, and his deep blue eyes. As I drifted off to sleep I could imagine staying with him suspended in a dreamland of Freudian id forever. When we woke up, we carved our pledges of love for each other on the roof of the cave with pieces of stone writing, "S.W. (heart's) L.L." and "L.L. (heart's) S.W." I showed him all of the petroglyphs on the rocks and canyon walls that I had found or that Supai friends had shown me. My favorite was a human skull that could only be seen on horseback or by climbing the tall black boulder that it was clearly etched upon in white. It was an eerie depiction of a common symbol of death yet it fascinated me. It was as though I had found a lost cultural treasure of long ago, an ancient message of some kind whose meaning died with its inscriber. Scott walked me to my house. We said our goodbyes and after that he tried to visit each weekend. Scott and I were back together and our feelings kept getting stronger toward one another. His smooth hot kisses stayed on my lips for sometimes weeks at a time.

December was an unforgiving month for the Havasupai that year. A married teaching couple and their children left suddenly, leaving teaching vacancies in the 6th and 7th grade classes. Their two youngest children had been physically assaulted by a group of Supai children. Their five-year-old had to have stitches where his head had been split open with a strike to the forehead by one of the attackers. The child was having recurring nightmares about the incident. The tribe failed to punish the children involved. The couple was told not to leave their children unattended in the yard in front of their rental home to prevent possible future incidents. The teachers, as non-Natives, had to pay cash for medical center treatment on the reservation, so the stitches cost the family hundreds of dollars with the doctor's fee and supplies. The former Marine, his wife, and sweet children had had enough of a run-around and left in protest with their pride intact. They were off to Sunflower, after experiencing such poor treatment that first cold week of December.

The weather quickly became chill-you-to-the-core cold. There was a foot or more of snow "up top" and reported ice on the trail. Hiking in these conditions could put a man in danger, or get him killed. There were plenty of freezing-to-death tales to go around on the reservation. They were interesting true stories of near-death and deadly encounters with winter weather by members of the tribe. The helicopter couldn't fly in the snowy icy cold weather. Three weekends came and went without any weekend transportation to hilltop. Like many others living in Supai, I wondered if my car was still there or if it would be able to start once I made it back up there. Tensions ran high in the village. Supplies were low in the general store, because shipments only came in once per week on Wednesdays if the helicopter was running. If a townsperson needed food or other necessities she had to hurry to buy the items during her lunch break because the weekend snow storm pattern wasn't letting up any time soon. Cabin fever was spreading throughout Supai. My roommates were going to hike out, ice or no ice, because they couldn't stand being trapped for more than three weeks. I agreed with them, but I insisted on staying at the house because another snowstorm was supposed to have already begun "up top". My librarian friend Lenore invited me over to her house for dinner on both Friday and Saturday night, knowing that I would be alone. She was a co-worker who was fun to work with and always gave excellent advice about many subjects. Her friendship meant a lot to me. She had been raised by an Anglo couple in Flagstaff until she turned eighteen. After attending college, she traced her roots back to the reservation where she received a warm welcome from her extended Havasupai family. She found work with the tribe and never left. Lenore filled me in on much of the folklore and history of the tribe. She lent me history books about the Havasupai, one of which still needs to get back to her, but I will give it to her in person. If it ever became lost in the mail, I'd never be able to forgive myself. Lenore's family was very solid. Her husband was a quiet, hardworking spouse and father. He helped to provide for Lenore and their children, as well as for the horses that he used for packing tourists and goods back and forth to the reservation. She and her husband still slept outside, even during the recent cold snaps. They had a full-sized bed under the stars behind their house. In a way, those were hardy and romantic accommodations even when the horse sounds were factored in. He told hilarious stories during and after dinner. They had purchased satellite television and a dish, so watching television at their home was a treat. We would put a funny show on and just laugh the night away with refreshments from Lenore's recipe book. She was an excellent cook. She made the fluffiest thick fry bread that melted in my mouth. The children got embarrassed by some of their father's colorful language and would shake their heads.

We were passing the shut-in weekend time together to minimize any cabin fever symptoms because it could make people do outrageous things. It was a fever that I didn't intend upon catching. Lenore and her family members always made me feel welcome. I would help Lenore cook in the kitchen, or help one of the children with their homework while Lenore got her housework done or talked on the phone long distance. It was my way of paying back Lenore and her family for their kindness and acceptance of me. Finally, the stormy weather was interrupted and there was a slight thaw. We would all be able to get out during the coming week. Most of us were thrilled because we were all running low on food and morale. The one casualty of the shut-in was the beating death of a relative of the school secretary, which involved alcohol and a woman. The woman was being sexually assaulted and her brother, the one who died, had tried to stop the accused from hurting his sister. The whole tribe was in mourning for the loss of a promising young man who was gallantly trying to keep his sister from being raped. It was a tragic death and so unnecessary. The cold-blooded accused killer sat at the jail, which was a caged pen that prisoners could look out of. Just knowing how dangerous that man was turned my stomach and sent chills up my spine. He had a blank stare and looked straight ahead in a kind of trance. The tribe would close the school the Monday after the murder, for a day of mourning and a day-long funeral.

The three of us Havasupai Elementary workers took a one-day sabbatical, cleaning our classrooms, eating lunch at the café, and hiking to Havasu Falls and back. As we walked back up to the house, the front door swung open oddly in the wind. The swinging front door exposed the open storm door where we saw our refrigerator tipped over in the center of the kitchen floor. Somebody had been in our house during the funeral. The refrigerator had been trashed. Our dishes had been smashed to pieces that were scattered on the kitchen floor. Our bag of flour was gone with a coating on the counters and linoleum floor that resembled a dusting of snow. We immediately ran to our bedrooms to check our duffel bags and closets for our valuables. The thief, or thieves, had stolen all of our clothes and blankets. Our personal hygiene items, including our toothpaste and deodorant, were gone. My makeup had vanished. They also stole my new, and only, pair of hiking boots. My roommates' things were also gone. I felt the worst for June. She had been robbed of a camera with a zoom lens that was a treasured gift from her father. June was devastated and angry tears poured down her cheeks as she lithely said, "They took everything that we cared about and needed, everything." Then she swore in Swahili, a language that she learned while a child living in Africa. She used Swahili to help discipline the school children. The booming Swahili instructions seemed to grab their attention until the Supai and English orders sunk in. I didn't know what she was yelling, but I'm sure it wasn't a prayer of forgiveness. We were very heated at being left without clothes, anything to keep warm with, or food to eat. The culprit had also spilled all of our beverages on the floor. It was an ungodly mess from the kitchen to the bedrooms and ended in the living room. Luckily, Mike had hid the record player and his albums well enough under a handmade cover, so we still had some entertainment. Our radio was broken into a bunch of tangled wiry fragments. The bean bags were knifed and beads were all over the floor. The overstuffed pillows had also been ripped apart into unrecognizable rags and scattered pillow stuffing. We discovered how the robber or robbers had gotten into the house. A person smashed a small window above the double-locked back door and squeezed through it to unlock the rest of the house. We had the feeling that whoever had done this operated quickly, had probably watched us leave, and broke in as soon as we were far enough up the trail for us not to hear or see them. We were tempted to go to the funeral if for no other reason but to see who may have had our clothes on in the crowd of mourners, but decided to call the police, instead. The tribal police sped over on their ATVs. The rookie BIA officer gave us official documents to list the stolen items on with their estimated worth. He took down notes about the scene and dusted for fingerprints as we spoke to the chief. He was going to look for witnesses as people came back from the funeral. He figured somebody in the neighboring homes had to have seen something. It had been the perfect opportunity for a crime: robbing a house while the rest of the tribe was at a funeral at the farthest end of the reservation away from the residential area. We figured that whoever it was who had done the crime had probably already climbed out of the canyon and would stay away. After our home was so violently destroyed and ransacked, we wondered if our personal safety was also at risk. We couldn't stop thinking what may have happened had we been there that morning. None of us wanted to be alone in the house after the robbery. We all thought of resigning, because the tribe couldn't guarantee our safety or the extra patrols by the house that we requested. The tribe promised financial compensation for the stolen items if a Havasupai tribe member had committed the crime, otherwise the tribe was not responsible. We understood the tribe's stance, but not the refusal to offer us extra security. For the rest of that week, we slept at the school. Thanks to Bill and Melinda Gates, we had movies and the internet for distraction. Plus, the school was warm and had a back-up generator if the power went out due to inclement weather, which it often did along with our telephone service.

Mike decided to stay at the reservation to pay back his federal student loans. He would repair the window and remove all of the rest of the valuables that weekend. He and June cleaned up their things and would replace them with inexpensive substitutes from the Goodwill. I locked my remaining clothes in my desk at school. June and I decided that we were unsafe without Mike's presence in the house. They would leave every weekend from then on. Hesitantly, I called Scott and my family to tell them what had happened. Scott offered his spare room until I found a new job and apartment. He said, "I love you and don't want to lose you just because you are stubborn and have too much of a big heart to be selfish. It's not safe down there, so just resign and get to Mesa where you won't have to live in fear." I didn't want to admit that it had become unsafe for me to be alone at the house after the recent escalation of violence among tribal members and then the house robbery. My mind was made up as soon as Mike and June were heading out of town on Friday afternoon. They asked if I needed something to protect myself with while they were gone. I didn't feel safe and it didn't look like the tribe was going to look after the house. Mike and June asked again for me to leave with them. They made it clear that they were not leaving me alone in the house. I decided to hike out with them.

Once I got to Scott's house in Mesa, I called my parents to tell them what happened. They were furious. My parents urged me to resign immediately. Dad's exact words were, "Pack up what's left of your things and get the Hell out of there before you're attacked, or worse." I knew Dad was right and so was my mother. Too many scary, but realistic, scenarios now ran through my mind. I was in danger of being harmed physically or ending up dead if attacked when I was alone in that house. I wrote a letter of resignation that weekend to the tribe that began with, "Please accept this letter of resignation as I no longer feel that the tribe can protect me or my personal belongings from further criminal acts," and continued to comment on the exact reasons for my departure. It was payday, so I went to Mr. Argus to pick up my last paycheck. He told me that he had spoken to Mrs. Champlain. He maliciously unleashed the following assault of his own, "It has come to my attention that you are resigning. Either you change your mind and rescind the letter or I will refuse the resignation and deny you your pay. You are looking for this, aren't you?" He then held up my paycheck, pretended to hand it to me, and deviously tore it up like scrap paper. It was the only thousand dollars that I had in this world and this lunatic had torn it up. I didn't say a word as I left his office.

I walked straight up to the tribal council offices. They told me to go to payroll with Mr. Argus and ask for another check in the amount that he had torn up. Mr. Argus refused to do it. Without money for the helicopter, I would have to leave my belongings behind. I trekked back to the house with my head hanging in defeat. I excused myself for interrupting their lunch break and told them what had happened. Mike said, "That rotten jerk! Grab your stuff and I'll meet you at the helicopter landing. Don't argue with me. Just do it. You are like a sister to me and nobody treats my sister this way!" He stormed out to return to the school. I felt horrible. My stomach sinks just thinking of the events of that fateful, heart-wrenching day. I was finished packing my things in the milk crate because my duffel bag was stolen in the robbery. Mike went to school and then to payroll. I had hoped for some good news, but he shook his head as he approached me while I was cleaning out my desk. Kat, my assistant, was beside herself and asked me to live with her because nobody would dare mess with her. My students came in from recess and hugged me so powerfully that none of us wanted to let go. Tyler, one of my most difficult students, my self-described "Half-breed" ran out of the room so that nobody could see him crying. They knew about the robbery and understood why I was leaving. The single father of one of my female students, Melanie, walked into the classroom. His plea effected me the most as he said, "My daughter has more confidence because of you. She sticks up for herself with the kids who tease her now. You are a mother figure to her. You're good with my daughter. You are good for the kids. Just stay for our kids." I could barely keep my composure as I saw Melanie's father wiping tears from his eyes. My heart was breaking for my students and the parents that stood in my classroom asking me to stay. One of the girls muttered, "You're quitting. You're no good, just like the rest of you Anglo teachers," as I walked by her desk to leave. I had run out of things to say. Everyone knew why I was leaving; they just hated the reality of the situation as much as I did. My dream of a peaceful Supai died during a tribal funeral. I had chosen my safety over my teaching position. The choice I was making was the only one that made any sense. My goal there had been to teach, not to perish in a state of denial. Many parents offered me emotionally-charged farewell wishes. They vowed to have Mr. Argus relieved of his duties at the next tribal council meeting. I hoped they would.

Mr. Argus was obviously unstable and worked to intimidate good teachers who were leaving the school month after month leaving vacancies that were tough to fill. He was costing the tribe's children a good education by not offering safe housing for teachers. The Havasupai chief apologized for the shortcomings of law enforcement there but said that the BIA controlled the number of assigned officers, not him. We shook hands. I thanked him for the once-in-a-lifetime opportunity to live with his people and to get to teach the Havasupai children which had been rewarding work. He told me that he hoped to see me someday under different circumstances. His words were, "You'll always be welcome here. You will not be easily forgotten by the Havasupai people. Take care of yourself."

Melanie's father waited for me outside the tribal office building. As I gathered my things, he grabbed my hand and pleaded, "Please don't go. I will guard your house myself. The kids need you. My daughter needs you. I will get a collection together to buy you new clothes and replace what was stolen. Please, Lara..," Then he just hugged me and quietly sobbed, which makes me tear up to this day, and whispered, "I wish you never got robbed and that we could keep good teachers like you. We're gonna miss you, teacher." Seeing that man in tears broke my heart. The reasons for my departure were no more his fault then they were mine. I was devastated.

I sensed that my future was "up top" in the Phoenix area near Scott, the man that I was so deeply in love with. I told Melanie's father to let his daughter know that I cared about her and the other children very much and would miss her. I assured him that Agnes Champlain would find another teacher as quickly as possible to complete the school year. It was time to walk to the helicopter field and say my goodbyes to villagers along the way. Fletcher passed me on the trail just past the general store. He hugged me saying into my ear, "If that Anglo boyfriend of yours ever treats you bad, tell him I'll hunt him down, OK?" We both laughed through some short-lived tears and walked away from each other in opposite directions. We turned around to watch each other until we were out of each other's sight. A raven sat in a tall tree branch overhead with something in its mouth. Havasupai folklore has it that if you pass a raven with food in its mouth you will soon come into money or good fortune. I needed that to be the case in my situation. I smiled as I thought of other folklore. Now I had to have a wolf or deer cross my path for good luck and an eagle feather to fall from the sky to give me strength. I didn't want to see a fox because that meant that someone would try to trick me and someone already had. The worst thing that could happen was for an owl to fly into your home because it meant that you, or someone close to you, would die. Luckily I had no home for the owl to fly into.

Bidding a fond farewell to Havasupai reservation's only bovine, I said, "Goodbye little cow." It was a runt that an elderly Supai woman planned on eating over the winter. Mike called the poor thing "hamburger helper." I wanted to take it with me so that it could be a free range cow "up top" with the rest of the creatures living along the BIA Route 18. I could hear the familiar sound of the helicopter in the distance. I was relieved to know that it was coming. Mike made it to the ticket stand just in time for me to pay my fare and say goodbye. He ran up to me, gave me a hug, and put a wad of cash in my hand which he and June felt I needed to make it to the valley of the sun. He was like a brother to me. I wondered when I would see him and his peppy future wife again. They were good people. I hope they live in a large house in Williams with a bunch of children, teaching them how to make music and create pottery. I told Mike to call me at Scott's house if he needed to get in touch with me.

After I left Supai, Mike called once to make sure I was alright. He told me that the money lent was a "friendship-related" investment not meant to be repaid in cash. Repayment of a life well-lived and well-loved was payment enough for him and June. I assured him that my relationship with Scott was going well and that I was enrolled at Arizona State University for my education coursework. I could almost see him smiling over the telephone. That was my last conversation with Mike. I hope he reads this book and looks Scott and me up. I would love to see him. Scott and I must return to Supai someday before it becomes too distant a memory.

I stayed with Scott a short time, getting two jobs. The first job was as a full-time activities assistant at a Christian retirement community in North Phoenix. It was a peaceful job in an upbeat senior community whose inhabitants knew how to live well throughout their golden years. It was an upscale senior luxury apartment complex. The residents enjoyed many outings to the theater, shopping, and fine dining, and taking scenic drives in the community's plush air conditioned vans. The dining at Christian Care was exquisitely orchestrated by a French sous chef. He would make me decadent artistic desserts-of-the-day to take home and left them on my desk before I left for the day. I led exercise routines as well as organized cultural and social events at the community. I would make arrangements for activities throughout the Phoenix metropolitan area and Arizona. We did chair aerobics to "Alley Cat." I can still hear the melody of that song, "Do do do do dodo dee do-do do do do do do" on the old-fashioned tape player.

One of my residents, a kind Italian man, brought me *pizzelle* every week with his "family initial" press. They were scrumptious. The women would make me little gifts such as bookmarks and knit goods. I was furniture-challenged at my Union Hills Avenue, Glendale, apartment away from Scott's procrastination and indecisiveness regarding marriage. The residents would bring me their old gadgets, kitchen utensils, pans, or furniture that was slated to be thrown or given away. The community's reverend demanded that I take an old Lazy Boy chair that was being thrown away. I told him that I had a third floor apartment. He told me that he would help me carry it all the way up himself because he insisted that I have it. A woman, who had summered with her family in Florida as a child, had many boxes of sea shells that her mother had colored and polished by hand. She was going to throw the shells away because nobody in her family wanted them. She wanted me to take a box. I used each one of those shells to create custom art photo frames for wedding favors.

Scott called me at my apartment to ask if he could give me some important mail related to taxes or something like that. I told him that my only free time was on Friday nights because I worked at Rawhide Western Town the rest of the weekend until it closed. Rawhide was an amusement park in North Scottsdale, an invented western town where street actors walked around and tended to visitors by helping at amusements such as the petting zoo, rock climbing wall, mechanical bull, sling shot ride, or haunted house. When performers weren't at an amusement, they acted a part. My self-developed character was Prudence, a Bible-thumping prude-about-town who would read Bible verses or shout things like "Look at these heathens," or "Jezebel!" to another actor who was a painted lady or saloon girl. I would also preach at people who cussed, committed public displays of affection, or looked like they were having too much fun. Sometimes I would have the town's sheriff arrest them and put the outlaws in jail. It was a lot of fun and I made decent money doing it. I wore floral print and gingham Laura Ashley and western-style full-length dresses that I had found at consignment stores. My cowgirl boots were brown suede and my accessories came from the actor's prop room. I made my own gaudy western hats using a lot of fabric flowers and a glue gun. My Rawhide co-workers were ornery, showy, and a lot of fun to work with and watch. The actors and stunt people were definitely Hollywood caliber, only many would never willingly leave Arizona. I admired their loyalty to Rawhide. The park eventually shut down for a short time, but re-opened at the Gila River Reservation's Wild Horse Pass Casino and Resort in Chandler, Arizona.

Friday night came. I was exhausted from both of my demanding jobs. I went to Padre Murphy's Irish Pub in Glendale, which was my favorite watering hole on Friday nights. I knew the regulars there on a first-name basis. Scott had agreed to meet me there when he got off of working at his interim auto parts sales job as he waited to be called by Caterpillar in Phoenix in regard to a better sales position with them. I told my bar friends that my ex-boyfriend was coming to bring me my mail. They thought it was so funny that they schemed up a plan for the unsuspecting Scott, who I still loved very much but had worked to get over in the six months that we had been apart. One of the guys was tall and large-framed with a beard and hair that made him resemble André the Giant of 1980s wrestling fame, who said in his deep voice, "When he gets here, introduce me as your boyfriend. Let me let him in on the punch line, OK?" It was definitely a "make him jealous" strategy that I was willing to participate in after his absence.

When he came in, I stood behind the bar with "André" and my pub friends. I was not about to rush up to see the person who took over half a year to decide that he had important mail for me.

I thought his excuse to see me was transparent and unoriginal. My first impulse was to ignore him completely in anger because I had almost completely accepted that he and I would never be together again. As I considered leaving, he suddenly recognized me from across the barroom near the front door where he stood. He looked awful. He looked exhausted and had gained a little weight since we had parted ways. He sometimes was a stress eater, so apparently the calming effect that I had on him while we were together was amiss. Scott's familiar sweet smile was a pleasant sight.

He was still the handsome man that I had loved the year before, with his intense blue eyes and platinum down-soft hair. He was wearing a short-sleeved white polo shirt and jeans that looked incredibly attractive with him in them. He asked if I had eaten. My friend at the bar piped in, "Hey buddy! What are you doing over there with my girl?" You should have seen Scott's face tense up at my phony boyfriend's question. Scott said, "I'm sorry, I didn't realize you had a boyfriend." When my buddy saw the look of disappointment on Scott's face, he caved. He explained, "Lara's not my girlfriend, but be good to her or you'll have to deal with *me*." Scott perked up and asked me again if I'd eaten. I told him that I had not, and we put our names in for a table on the restaurant side for a little privacy.     Scott sat on one side of the table with me on the other. My defenses were in high gear. My sixty-plus hour workweek didn't allow me much time for energy or a sense of humor, especially where commitment-phobe Scott was concerned. I let him do the initial talking because I was ready to bite his head off for bothering me after six months of not a word. I had obliterated him from my everyday thought processes and felt good about that. *How dare he get in touch with me after over half a year?! Who did he think he was, my soulmate or something?*

Scott told me that I looked good. I told him that I swam two hours every night, ate close to nothing, and didn't have time to sit around and think about men, much less him. Instead of taking offense, he became proactive by asking to sit next to me on my side of the table. I told him, "I suppose you can if you don't want to shout over the table." Then, I sighed and rolled my eyes as I contemplated whatever groveling might come next. He persisted by asking if he could hold my hand. I thought to myself, *I don't hate you. You just waited too long to let me know what you've been thinking.* I held out my hand matter-of-factly. He squeezed my hand saying, "I missed holding this hand." Then he kissed it. His touch was making me melt inside.

I sat on the bench stone-faced. My affections would not be toyed around with as easily as the year before. The new and improved Lara could take or leave any man with ease. He then did the unthinkable by asking to kiss me. I moved my cheek toward him. He said, "I guess I should have been more specific. I meant 'on the lips.'" He leaned in toward me to kiss me and I let him. We kissed a long, long time until the server came over to the table and jokingly said, "I guess I don't have to ask how you two are doing." Once we realized who she was talking to, we both turned bright red and laughed. My butterflies were back.

Scott and I hadn't fallen out of love with each other. There was an even more powerful connection between us than before our break-up. I never let my guard down after our reunion night. My goal was to play hard-to-get. Scott had to come see me on my terms, not his. If he wanted to see me on the weekends, it would only be if I didn't have other plans. I wasn't ready to give him a free pass back into my life. He wasn't getting exclusive dating rights, either. I had an active dating life and this time around I wanted to be sure that Scott's admissions of love were sincere.

The other men that I was dating were a diverse group of characters. I liked to go to plays and movies with a professional stunt man from Rawhide that enjoyed them as much as I did. There was a defense attorney whose short stature and mother's decorative touches at his home turned me off romantically. He was a very good person, extremely devoted to the Silent Witness program, and he was a lively conversationalist. I liked his company and he had great taste in restaurants. The food was divine, even if the chemistry wasn't. The other, more-of-a-friend-than-a-date, was a gorgeous Brazilian immigrant in his early twenties who enjoyed swimming with me in the pool whenever he saw me doing my laps. I would teach him basic English phrases which I knew would get him ahead in the United States. He would bring me flowers and kept me company in the pool area. Every week, my Brazilian friend would replace my old roses with a dozen new ones. Last, but not least, was an older teacher who wasn't far from retirement at the Phoenix Preparatory Academy whom I met after my successful interview that summer. He played piano beautifully, took me for long drives in his convertible, and everyone who knew him was enamored with him. We enjoyed each other's company. His neighbors looked skeptically at the older teacher dating the younger one, but we didn't care. To me, age has always been just a number. He had never had children with his first wife and was looking for a woman who wanted to get married and have children. Scott had competition. He would have to wait patiently to get any of my precious weekend time. My theory was that he took six months to make a decision that I might be "the one." I would take at least six months to let him know where I stood, which was only appropriate under the circumstances.

Little by little, I found myself falling back in serious love with Scott in every aspect. The men that I had been dating had one or two of the many qualities that I looked for in a man. Scott had everything that I had always looked for in a mate. He was fiercely competitive like me. He had a strong commitment to family which I, too, possessed. He took care of himself and his appearance which was important to me. We shared political views and had the same family values. We were about the same age. I liked that he was a little taller than I was because the attorney that I had been dating only met me at chest level which made me feel uncomfortable.

Scott was romantic without being fallacious. I had found little pieces of Scott's character traits in men that I dated. Scott was all of those pieces glued together to create the soulmate that I had always dreamed of yet had never found before he entered my life. When Scott and I got together on the weekends, we had a lot of fun. We hiked, went to concerts, and went dancing with our friends. We both had difficulty saying goodbye. Both of us were wondering if the other was in this for the long haul.

One night Scott kissed me goodnight in the doorway of my apartment before he left for the night. He had only been gone for a few minutes when I heard knocking on my door. It was Scott, standing outside my door with a look of concern on his face. He explained that when he went to the parking lot his car was gone. His Infiniti had been stolen. What a date! Imagine dropping your date off, kissing goodnight, and then finding that your car had been stolen! I felt horrible. I invited him back in to call the police and his insurance company. The insurance company paid for a rental car. Scott couldn't stand going from his luxury sedan to a clunky rental car because it was a bit rickety, making a "tinny" sound when we drove over pebbles. It had slow acceleration which was fine unless you're like Scott and I. We both enjoy a lot of horsepower under the hood. His car turned up a month later with only minor damage and a Phoenix public library music CD in it. His car had most likely been "borrowed" by a group of teenagers, the authorities told us, because none of the fingerprints were on file.

Scott and I went to Flagstaff and Sedona on our dates because we both loved to hike. Some of the most beautiful forests, trails, and other amazing natural sights were in northern Arizona. Our favorite hiking place was through the red rocks of Sedona, Arizona. We enjoyed taking relaxing dips at red rock crossing or in Oak Creek. Wading in Oak Creek was especially refreshing after a hot, sweaty hike. Oak Creek instantly smoothes hooves of any human or other animal variety. There were Native American jewelry stands on weekends along Oak Creek on the scenic 89A near the big Dairy Queen. Sometimes, before winter came, we would see Navajo or other native tribe members selling their handmade crafts throughout northern Arizona. I have bought jewelry at the Little America hotel, where John Kerry has stayed, or at other popular Flagstaff venues. Grand Canyon National Park is another excellent place to buy handcrafted Native American items directly from the person who made the piece or pieces. Sedona is a place with a multitude of artistic and sensory indulgences that visitors have to pace themselves to truly enjoy. It is a magical place where natural healers, psychic readers, and many New Age aficionados make a living by intriguing and pampering Sedona's visitors. Sedona doesn't need any of these distractions to be a pleasing destination. There was a calming energy that is almost tangible there. The stargazing was the best I have ever experienced outside of the Grand Canyon. Even when the tourist season was in high gear I could still find peaceful quiet in nature, either on foot or horseback. Vistiors can go on a Jeep tour or an aerial tour of the red rocks if they are unable or unwilling to hike. The gorgeous city was named for Sedona Schnebly, a pioneer wife who was the first boarding house owner and school teacher. She was disowned by her WASP-y parents who did not approve of her selection of a working class husband. Her husband, T.C. Schnebly ran a successful freight-hauling business between Flagstaff and the area. He named the city for his beloved wife when the postmaster asked him to come up with a name for the beautiful place that they had helped settle. Scott and I went to Sedona as often as we were able.

I began my new teaching position teaching eighth grade language arts in downtown Phoenix at the Phoenix Preparatory Academy. It was a uniform public school that was two stories high and had a huge, exciting, and diverse student population. It was difficult going until a veteran teacher named Sandi took mercy on my new teacher status. Sandi took me under her wing. She scolded both my students and me until I had full control over the discipline in my classes.

Sandi's classroom management style was second to none. She knew how to engage the students in their lessons and how to get results. Like many teachers, she detested standardized tests which she thought punished children from non-English-speaking and low-income households. Most of the standardized tests she said were geared toward middle-to-upper-class students who had grade level, or better, grasps of the English language, unlike many inner city students who grow up where there is a high number of immigrant children. I learned quickly that Sandi was correct on her assessment of the standardized assessments our teacher evaluations were greatly effected by.

I was learning a lot about how our society values, or devalues, inner city children who are at-risk in the educational arena. As a social worker, I could navigate through the red tape to get children what they needed to live better. As a teacher, I was responsible for the direct education of the all important language skills and other skills that can greatly affect your students' futures. Is teaching a high pressure job? You bet it is. Most of my students were a few years below grade level, as though not much progress had been made since sixth grade. These were the children that I immediately placed on the Accelerated Reader Program. The program allowed children to read independently and get tested for comprehension until they reached grade level proficiency at a rapid pace.    My students were always learning in a highly structured, but never rigid, classroom environment. These children had a lot of anxiety and frustration that needed both venting and eradication. I focused on a lot of grammar and speech because many of my students were weak in these areas. Several of my students in each class were new to the United States from Central and South America, as well as Mexico. These kids deserved a shot at the American Dream, which I believe begins with mastery of the English language. Students amazed me year after year with their above-average abilities to meet grade level challenges, even when they had started the year at a grade level language ability disadvantage.

Scott visited me on lunch breaks when he could at "the Prep," bringing takeout or taking me to a nearby restaurant for a quick bite to eat. My students teased me about getting married. It was touching to have my students so concerned about their teacher when I was acutely concerned about their levels of language proficiency. Scott's office was close to the school, so we would meet with his and my co-workers for happy hour on Friday afternoons. The teachers at the Prep were a fun crew. We had so much fun together at work and at play. They were like a second family to me. When you are an educator, you have to have a strong, close-knit team or else you and your students suffer. We always stuck together both on and off the clock. It is sad when I hear a teacher say that his or her co-workers lack unity.

Luckily, I have not experienced disunity at the schools where I taught. Students deserve stability from the school board on down in my opinion. Those who do not believe that providing a stable safe environment for students is a priority for effective learning should not be in the teaching profession. Our nation's students deserve a commitment that is enduring and sincere in terms of providing a public education that produces graduates who can compete locally and globally in our workforce.

Once the children knew that I was happy to be teaching them in preparation for high school success, my classes were calm and highly-productive. I made myself available during lunch break and after school for any of the children who needed extra help with anything taught in class or with a homework assignment. Many of my students' parents worked days and parts of the night at low-wage jobs to provide for their children. These parents did not have the luxury of being able to help their kids with their homework or help them with language concepts on a regular basis. The income gap can create a learning gap. Our job at the Preparatory Academy was to narrow the socioeconomic education gap in a student's favor. Parents appreciate teachers who work with a child's individual needs. When teachers or administrators blindly judge inner city parents and inject labels such as "unaffected" or "apathetic," that is when parents become angry and shut themselves off to the school. The last thing I wanted was for parents to distance themselves from their child's education or school.

Not many children's parents could come for conferences because of family and work responsibilities. One of my single moms was tired of her daughter's bad attitude, came in to see me, and told her pretty, rebellious daughter, "I don't clean up stinking garbage at the Diamondbacks stadium for you to talk back to your teacher and not try your hardest at school. You are too smart to clean up after people like I have to do because I didn't finish school. Don't you get it? Your mother cleans garbage off the floor and seats because I am lucky that they hire drop-outs. I was lucky!" She apologized for her daughter's disrespectful and self-defeating behavior. I wish all parents were this supportive of the school system. My single parents checked in on their students' progress frequently which pleased me because there was excellent cooperation on their end. Most married parents could at least be counted on for attendance at conferences. Parental involvement makes teaching a lot more effective because the parents were on the same page as their student. Reinforcement of skills that he or she was learning in class, in the student's home, was crucial to retention and strengthening of English language skills. The holidays were rapidly approaching. My teaching evaluation had gone well. New teachers usually never got a perfect review. Administrators would mark at least one category as "developing" to keep you aiming for educator perfection for next year's evaluation. What every teacher really wanted to see back from the principal was every column filled with the following comments, "Educator meets and exceeds goals and objectives." It was the stuff that new teacher's dreams were made of. It also got teachers bonus pay, lead teacher assignments, and fringe benefits that come in handy at any school district.

*Chapter Fourteen* ───────────────────────────

How do you reset this panic
button on my alarm system?

Scott asked me to go up to Sedona for Christmas Eve night. He had arranged a babysitter for his son. He told me that we would be going to Sedona to relax, enjoy the art galleries, and do some hiking. It sounded like a great break from the hustle and bustle of the Phoenix area. Scott drove around to every hilltop in Sedona, I suppose in an attempt to keep me guessing. He had a nervous expression on his face. He was sweating buckets as he kept rolling the window down to let the cool breeze hit his face. I asked if he felt alright. He looked as though he could pass out or something. I asked if he wanted to stop the car and hike, but he said "No. I don't want to hike here. Let's go." I tried to lighten up the situation by telling Scott, "Let's hurry up because that sun isn't going to wait for us to find the perfect hiking spot." He looked frustrated, which was not common for Scott. It had dawned on me that he may be looking for a place to propose to me, so my internal panic alarm began to sound off with a loud "Thump! Thump!" as my heart began to race. My face was most likely bright red and felt hot.

Was he actually going to propose, or simply drive us around in circles until the next appropriate activity of star gazing could be enjoyed? He turned in toward Chapel Rock and parked the car in some gravel brush next to the closed entrance. It was past five o'clock, so no more visitors could park on the church property. He was irritated because there were other hikers. He obviously wanted some serious privacy for some reason. Scott had been pacing on the red rock outcroppings beneath the beautiful cross of Chapel Rock when he suddenly fell to one knee and grabbed my hand. He mentioned how he loved me too much to ever consider living without me. He told me that there was no other Lara out there. Then he popped the question in his own beautiful way, which will remain our secret. My soulmate and I would be husband and wife. That may sound old-fashioned to some, but we were absolutely in our love with each other, unlike in past relationships that we had both gladly departed. I can't explain how happy I was at that moment, only that I felt a sense of relief. I readily accepted his long-awaited proposal.

We were engaged on Christmas Eve, 2001, at the base of Chapel Rock in Sedona, Arizona, as the sun was setting on the horizon. We had an unforgettably-romantic dinner with incredible entrees and desserts at a fine dining establishment called Judy's on Soldier's Pass Road near Coffee Pot Rock in Sedona. We sat at a cozy table in front of a roaring fireplace. We were two go-getters, ready to take on the world one day at a time for the rest of our lives.

*Chapter Fifteen* ——————————————

Any product that claims it lasts
forever better have a lifetime warranty.

Scott and I decided to get married in July. We decided to forego a June wedding because it was too cliché. I was no blushing bride, and I wanted to get married in Rhode Island where most of my family lives. The venue was a choice that I had made well before meeting Scott. When I was fifteen years old, I got my first restaurant job as a busgirl at the Shelter Harbor Inn, an upscale bed and breakfast, with a restaurant, in Westerly. I had witnessed a lot of weddings through the dining room windows of the inn as a teenager, fantasizing about getting married someday in the gorgeous English style garden behind the inn. Immediately after we told our families about our engagement, I called to find out what days were available that summer. I not only got dates, but meal plans, and a DJ recommendation as well. My friend Jeff was still managing special events at the inn and was restaurant manager. It was a pleasant journey into the past when I heard his familiar voice saying, "So, Lara's getting married and wants to get married here? That's wonderful. Congratulations. I can't wait to see you all grown up. Gosh, you're making me feel old. I will let you know the dates that are available in July. Pick one and call me back as soon as possible so we can get started. No worries."

Our next goal was to find a Christian minister or Christian justice of the peace. Catholic priests, as you may know, do not do outdoor wedding ceremonies or location weddings, therefore we had to make sure that it remained a Christian ceremony. We eventually found a Catholic Justice of the Peace who could officiate the ceremony using both traditional and non-traditional music and vows. Nobody was going to play a traditional wedding march like the overused "Here Comes the Bride" at my wedding. I would walk down the aisle to Enya's "Flora's Secret," which was a lot more romantic and told of the kind of deep passion that Scott and I felt for each other. The traditional wedding march, from my feminist perspective, speaks to bondage and a contrived purity that first-time brides are supposed to embody. I was not giving up my feminist core values to get married.

It was the beginning of a strong partnership with a powerful love and devotion that was refreshingly mutual. The word "obey" was never part of our vows because we did not believe that we should dominate or oppress one another. We were a team. Team members do not order each other around or make demands that are meant to make someone submissive. Patriarchy would not rear its ugly head in our marriage or our home. Indentured servitude does not a marriage make. Those in a marriage should not have to "obey" each other. Those who willingly choose to be dominated shouldn't complain unless they are willing to try to escape an oppressive, self-destructive relationship or marriage.

We called Jeff back and chose to get married on Saturday, July 6, 2002, immediately after one of my favorite holidays, Independence Day. I wanted my marriage to be tied in with the fireworks, patriotism, and a reminder of independence as a concept that was a continually-important factor in my perception of success in life. The invitations were ready shortly after. The RSVPs came in quickly. There would be a small wedding with approximately one hundred guests comprised of close friends and family members. There would be no Rolls Royce, stretch limos, or any over-the-top extravagant wedding party. My wedding would be like a small-scale cotillion. It would be sophisticated, entertaining, pleasing-to-the-palate, and practical. My matron of honor was my married best childhood friend Jen. Jen is gorgeous, hilarious, and we have been there for each other throughout every one of our major life transitions. The bridesmaid would be Alice, a close friend of mine from high school who had been an Elite agency sports model in New York City during our first few years of college at the University of Rhode Island. She was pretty and had a biting wit. The flower girl would be Jen's exceptionally adorable little girl, Katie, in a dress that Jen's mother had adorned with silk flowers. The ring bearer would, appropriately, be my eleven-year-old stepson Devin. Scott's best man was Tommy, a dark sunglasses-wearing close friend of ours who was a stylish, kind-hearted, self-employed rebellious inactive LDS (or Latter Day Saints) member, and a complete hoot, from Surprise, Arizona. My brother was an usher who was thrilled to be escorting a former sport's model, Alice, down the aisle. The wedding party was complete and the guest list was ready. We hired a moderately-priced DJ, because Scott and I couldn't stand scary wedding singers or bad wedding music. Our photographer was a woman named Sandra, a new photographer out of Providence, who had a great website and extraordinary portfolio. Sandra was new, but had an incredible gift in her photographic talent. The photos are magical to gaze upon. She was friendly and focused on making the event a success and planned on enjoying herself. That is what you want in a professional photographer, not a Type-A demagogue who barks orders all day as I had seen at other weddings for a higher cost and a lot of un-needed aggravation. I would go with a new photographer again. She was a big hit and her work was top of the line.

 My parents helped pay for the extravagant flowers and food because they wanted me to have the wedding of my dreams, which was thoughtful and very generous of them. The roses that I selected were lavender and white. Lavender is my favorite color, so it would be the primary color at the wedding. The bride's maid's and matron's bouquets, dresses, men's boutonnière corsages, my bouquet, and accents on the guest's tables had lavender roses and silver confetti or silver baubles on them. My best friend Jen and I, armed with sizzling hot glue guns, had late night wedding favor assembly sessions to create the personalized seashell-decorated picture frames. The centerpieces that we made had sand and colored seashells on the bottom of fish bowls, with floating lavender candles on top once they were filled with water. Tommy had brought us the entire Charlestown Beach in a bag for the centerpieces, so we all had a good laugh. I never knew if he had done something accidentally, or just wanted to completely overwhelm me with some serious laughter. Everything was coming together as Scott's family arrived from Arizona. Scott's parents and sister stayed at a hotel not far from Shelter Harbor Inn. Scott, Devin, and Tommy were sharing a room at the Sea Breeze Motel.

The only crisis that came up before the wedding was a depressing phone call from my Catholic high school friend Alice whose personal life was a complete mess. She called me the day before the wedding rehearsal to let me in on the fact that she couldn't make it and to have someone else take her place. Alice had made an unlivable mess out of her life thanks to drugs and alcohol. These two "residuals" from the New York modeling world had cost her a reputation and a car. When she agreed to be in my wedding, she left out the part about becoming a complete disaster and a manipulative hack. *Who on God's green Earth did she think she was?* She had lied to me about her situation and was trying to ditch her friendly obligations. All she had to do was throw a dress on, stand still for about thirty minutes, eat some great food, and make merry. I told her that I didn't care what was going on. Unless she was physically ill, she had better show up in twenty-four hours or I would never speak to her again. She said she would get there. I abruptly hung up the phone. I was so disappointed in Alice's lack of self control. Thanks to many extra efforts to get her there, she made it to the rehearsal and wedding. While she was there, she mercilessly hit on my unsuspecting brother who fell for her sob story, hook, line, and sinker. And, not long after, they were married. Their marriage and the black cloud she had over her head didn't last beyond a year's time. Thankfully, for my brother's sake, she could not hide her true colors for very long. My new (and improved) sister-in-law is a great mother, has an excellent career, is refreshingly level-headed, and down-to-Earth. She and my brother are very happy and have a gorgeous little boy together who "Aunty Lara" loves to spoil. I only wish that my brother had been spared Alice's lies and mistreatment.

Our wedding day was picture perfect. Jen had researched a sand pouring ritual that added a welcome twist to our nuptials. All of our guests showed up on time. The food was delectable, but we didn't get time to eat much of it with all of the excitement of the day. The chairs were perfectly situated. The floral archway in front of the flowering garden was surreal. It was time to tie the knot to officially celebrate our strong love for one another that is still growing today. Ron, my professor mentor, was there with his wife. Friends from college, and most of my extended family members, were there.

The DJ played our hand-selected songs at the appropriate times. The only cliché song was the typical wedding recessional which we barely heard anyway in our ecstatic fugue of wedded bliss. The only scary part of the wedding was Scott's wobbling because he seemed weak-kneed as he was slipping the ring on my finger. I thought he might pass out, but he stayed strong. He quickly recovered and it was a humorous reminder of our hot steamy July day wedding at Shelter Harbor Inn.

The wedding was fun and so was the reception. Scott and I enjoy throwing a great party. We cut the cake to one of our favorite Sonny and Cher songs, "I got you Babe." We made a mess of the momentarily-flawless fresh purple flowers and greenery on the top of that cake.   Thank God for strategic wedding photography. Scott and I had photos taken at East Beach in Charlestown, Rhode Island. Let me just say for the record that walking in eighty-degree heat in an abundantly-beaded, sequined bodice designer Lazaro gown with thirty layers of generously-sequined tulle skirt in two-inch silver and rhinestone heels was no day at the beach. I had my rhinestone tiara on and a multi-layer handmade custom veil flippety-flapping in the ocean breeze, which wasn't easy on the photo-ops. The photo shoot only lasted around twenty minutes. We then rushed back to our guests to say "hello" and "goodbye" to those who had to leave early. As soon as our last guests left the inn, we were off to my parents' house to quickly change into non-wedding attire and get a ride from Tommy and Jen to catch our jet to Nevis Island, a Caribbean island in the West Indies. We stayed at Nisbet which is a gorgeous seaside resort on a secluded part of the island. Before we caught our first jet, I saw a familiar face. It was Rhode Island boxing legend Vinny Pazienza. I had loved to watch him box in his prime. I said hello and introduced myself and Scott to him. He wished us congratulations on getting married and yelled after us, "You kids have fun!" It was beyond cool to meet Vinny "Paz" in person. We caught our USAir flight for Pennsylvania, then on to Puerto Rico, and finally to the island hopper planes which would get us to our honeymoon island. The stewardess on our first flight out of Rhode Island saw the flowers in my hair and leis around our necks, so she made a big deal by having the flight's passengers give us a round of applause. The flight's pilot gave us complimentary champagne throughout the flight to Philadelphia. Scott and I, both exhausted, felt we had earned the praise. I was relieved to have my close-to-twenty-pound Lazaro gown and accessories off, no matter how much I adored them. We were relieved to be heading for Nevis Island, a non-tourist trap honeymoon destination.

You may be wondering why Scott and I chose Nevis Island, a lesser-known Caribbean island nation in the West Indies. The first, and most important, reason was that the last place we wanted the location of our honeymoon to be was in a tourist mecca. Secondly, Scott and I are privacy seekers. The last, and perhaps quirkiest reason, was the name of Nevis's capitol, which is Charlestown, the same name as my old hometown. A lot of celebrities have vacationed in Nevis to get away from annoying crowds. Sarah Jessica Parker and her husband Matthew Broderick, Oprah Winfrey, and Britney Spears have all vacationed there. We found out at the Nevis historical society that the accomplished actress Cicely Tyson's family was from Nevis. She is a local heroine because of all of the assistance she has given to the islanders. Nevis was made famous in 1778 for its healing hot spring bath house during British colonization times. The island produced a lot of sugar as well in its dark days of slavery in now-abandoned sugar mills. As an independent nation it has thrived as a wonderful destination for the world's eco-adventure enthusiasts and sun seekers to vacation.

Nisbet resort offers many activities and excellent multi-course meals, as well as an English-style afternoon tea with scrumptious finger sandwiches and pastries. Almost every bit of the food served was native to the island, unless someone requested otherwise. My favorite was the delicious rich spinach-green Kalaloo soup. I liked the wild sounding name. It had the smoothest texture and mouthwatering locally-grown fresh seasonings in it. When we relaxed on the beach, it was as though we were the only two people spending time with the gorgeous sweet-smelling tropical flowers, crabs, brown pelicans, free ranging goats, and the island's somewhat Jersey-looking cows. We went snorkeling in crystal clear water a little under a mile offshore at a reef. The boat captain's name was Lennox. He was a bit mischievous, trying to tease the snorkelers into enjoying the open bar as he sped to the snorkeling location. He had very good musical tastes, although some of the older tour attendees were unimpressed with the modern dance beats and heavy bass.

We hiked part of the rainforest of Nevis Mountain where we saw wild boars and heard monkeys chattering from their shelters in the rain. On the rainforest eco-tour, we enjoyed fresh mangos directly from the tree and learned a quick way to get the milk out of a coconut with a stick or screwdriver. The owner of the tour company was an American ex-patriot with a biology degree who vacationed with his wife there and never left. Scott and I can understand why someone would never want to leave. We felt the same way when our week-long vacation came to an end. Nevis was a quiet, exotic place to visit.

Nevis celebrity gossip was very rich. Rumors abounded about Oprah's stays at the Four Seasons without leaving the confines of her Four Seasons room to mingle with the locals, which had offended some islanders. Our tour guide told us that the real reason Oprah was criticized was because she hadn't given autographs and many Nevisians idolized Oprah. I believe that Oprah probably just wanted to unwind with some privacy, peace, and quiet. Britney Spears, another guest at Nevis's Four Seasons hotel offended islanders because, although she signed autographs, she received too much attention which interfered with daily life on Nevis. Other Four Seasons guests and islanders alike were disgusted with the paparazzi and mobs at the hotel, throughout the island, and on Pinney's normally peaceful white sand beach. Apparently Britney had caused traffic jams much like during her Los Angeles, California, outings. I never would have guessed she was a media addict. The islanders really liked Matthew Broderick and Sarah Jessica Parker because they quietly mingled with the locals, kept to themselves, didn't cause traffic jams, gave autographs and posed for photos with islanders that they met.

Patterson, Nisbet's *maître d'* filled us in on island folklore and Nevis's local hot spots. He had the most interesting and spectacular necktie collection that I have ever seen. Patterson's ties came from all over the world. He made everyone at the resort feel special. He recommended the hippest restaurants and night clubs, which we appreciated. He took us to a local club for some dancing and cultural immersion. We met the famous Nevisian entertainer and restauranteur ,Sunshine, a cheerful man who mixed up "killer bee" rum punch drinks and, arguably, the island's best grilled food such as chicken and many kinds of barbequed food items. Sunshine was handsome, looked like a professional weightlifter, and had a fabulous full head of perfectly dreadlocked hair. Sunshine shook my husband's hand and said, "Welcome to matrimony, mon." Sunshine, Patterson, Scott and I talked, danced, and drank until early the next morning. We had been blessed by Sunshine, a Nevisian cultural icon. I look forward to getting back to Nevis for an anniversary trip.

As we left Nevis to return to our normal routines, we had a male customs agent stop us at the customs window. He said, "I have to tell you two something." We asked what it was. He said, "You are pregnant with a little girl." I was surprised and shocked by his forwardness and for making such an off-the-cuff presumption. Scott and I looked at each other and grinned, recounting that it was one of the strangest moments of our marriage. We brushed the "psychic" customs agent's remarks off. He and some island women at the airport explained that when a woman gets prettier and glows, then she is pregnant with a girl. If the woman has bad skin and looks unattractive, then she is probably having a boy. Little did we know at the time that the customs agent was correct on both the pregnancy and baby girl fronts. I wanted to find the Nevisian customs agent to see if he could guess the gender of the next child we may have to see if he could guess correctly twice. It was a long post 9/11 trip island hopping to St. Kitts, then on to Puerto Rico, where the security wait was so long that we had to take another flight the following day. We were ready to get back to the United States and to make our home in Mesa, Arizona. I was more than ready to adjust to married life and to start a new school year with another great group of students to educate and get to know.

*Chapter Sixteen*

I have the best tools for the job.
Don't tell me that I can't do it!

What skills will you need to reach your goal, the one thing that is most important for you to accomplish? For example, is it that you want to become a parent, but you are a single man or woman? Instead of focusing on the potential barriers to parenthood, call an agency that deals with adoption, foster parenting, or artificial insemination, for starters. If you exude determination, others will see it and help you reach your goal. Once you have made a list of items necessary to achieve parenting, begin taking steps to prepare yourself to do so. For example, if your home is too small, try to locate an affordable larger living space. In addition, let everyone in your support network know that you plan on becoming a parent. Once your dream becomes known to others close to you, it becomes more attainable as support builds for your goal. Create your tool kit. If you are having a difficult time finding the tools that you need, ask a professional or another parent who is supportive of you.

I know firsthand how rewarding parenting is. Ask any man or woman who has children how they got there. It is more complex than a fertilized egg, as we all know. Is there a successful parent who you are friends with, or a family member who can relate to your current situation? Before I had ever been in the situation that I personally wanted to be in before having children, doctors told me in my early twenties that I would probably never have children. They topped off this information by stating that I would possibly die trying because, medically, carrying a child full-term would most likely be impossible for me. As a woman who loves children and hoped to have my own some day, hearing those words from two highly-respected physicians just about crushed my hopes of ever becoming a biological mother. *How dare they destroy my dream of motherhood?* I never truly let myself believe what they had told me. At that moment, I decided that when the time came I would try everything possible to do the *im*possible, letting nothing and no one get in my way.

I discovered that I was, indeed, pregnant in 2002. I created a tool kit for motherhood. The first thing that I did, as soon as I finished telling my husband, was to call specialists in the field of high-risk pregnancy. I not only found out that the previous emergency room doctors were mistaken, but that I definitely could have children with appropriate medical intervention. It took the reassurance of these specialized high-risk obstetric professionals, who had excellent rates of success, to get rid of the emotional blockage from my past in regard to my potential motherhood. I was so happy, and equally scared, the day when I found out that I was pregnant. It was time to make a list of steps I had to take to maintain my health and the health of my unborn child. Only time would tell if medicine and my body would operate properly to keep me from losing my child to miscarriage. I found an obstetrician who was familiar with high-risk pregnancy. She immediately referred me to a perinatal high-risk specialist who would handle medication and specialized tests. He helped to ease my mind of all of the frightening predictions made by doctors in the past and helped me move forward. I developed a newfound confidence regarding the task at hand: maintaining myself and my baby to full-term.

The first thing that I had to do was to tell my closest family, friends, and co-workers what was happening. This was no easy task.

The last thing that I wanted to do was to scare those closest to me with news of a high-risk pregnancy. They were all very happy for my husband and me, yet very fearful for us and our unborn child. My doctors told me that my first three months were critical to a successful pregnancy. They told me to limit my life stress, take care of myself, and to give myself injections twice per day religiously for the next nine months to keep myself and my baby alive.

I will never forget the first time that I injected myself with one of the pre-filled syringes. I kept putting the needle on the skin of my belly fat and tried to press hard enough to break the skin. I pressed harder and harder. It really hurt. Plus, there was something about putting a foreign object such as a needle into any part of my body. I felt sick to my stomach. Tears were welling up in my eyes. Why couldn't I stick that needle in and push the medicine into my body? It was time to call my mother. Mom was a registered nurse with many years of experience. She would know the best way to give myself this injection. Scott couldn't bring himself to do it. He told me that he didn't want to inflict any pain on me. I told him that since I was pregnant that he was already too late for that. My mother told me to get an ice pack to numb the injection site, then to quickly inject myself. After giving myself the injection, she said to put the ice pack back on the injection site to minimize bruising. With the wisdom that Mom imparted to me, I managed to complete my first of many injections. They became just one more thing that I had to do to keep my baby and myself alive.

It was no easy task telling my school's principal that, for the remainder of the school year, I would be missing some of my teaching time for mandatory doctors' appointments to keep my body strong for the duration of my pregnancy. I was fortunate to have an understanding principal that allowed me to have the school counselor substitute in my afternoon classes when I had to leave for medical tests and other maternity-related doctor appointments. It worked out well because my students worked on their language skills and emotional issues when the counselor was there.

I had my first miracle when Sedona was born during Scott's and my first year of marriage. I found out that I have an unusual tolerance for pain. I was in active labor the day before I was scheduled to be induced with severe pain and loss of breath, also known as contractions. Although I was in a lot of pain, I would just sit down wherever I could at the stores during my last-minute baby shopping excursions. My friends always get a good laugh when I tell that story. Not even severe labor pains could keep me from hitting the sales.

I had beaten the pregnancy odds and produced a healthy child while preserving my own well-being. My second child, Eva, followed two years later, although with some medical complications. I was on the edge of gestational diabetes. It was a scary time late into my second pregnancy when I was concerned for my unborn child's health and my own. My body wasn't doing everything it was supposed to, and that got me frustrated. During labor, I became too weak to push any further, the baby's heart rate indicated fetal distress, and the doctor had to suction my baby out. She temporarily had a cone-shaped head. I learned a valuable lesson about how not to self-prescribe too much pain medication. You never know when the baby will decide that it's time to make its debut outside of your body. Unfortunately, because of the medication, I couldn't feel any pain. In my comfortably-numb condition, I couldn't feel whether or not I was pushing when the doctor and nurses told me to. Luckily none of the complications caused permanent harm to me or my child.

This is just another example of a time in my life when I met a goal using a set of tools to assure success, instead of operating blindly within a given situation like so many of us do. I had been told in my early twenties to never attempt to have children. Finding out that I was pregnant was simultaneously frightening and thrilling. My pregnancy would be high-risk. Scott and I got a second opinion as we searched for the best high-risk pregnancy specialists. We had the best high-risk pregnancy team imaginable. They turned a scary situation into a very well monitored healthy pregnancy, not once but twice. Scott and I will always be thankful for Doctors Messer and Garbaciak, as well as their cheerful staff members, during those exciting first years of our marriage. How different the two pregnancies had been.

*Why didn't I succumb to outdated medical advice from doctors that were present for my blood clot and transient ischemic attacks years earlier?* As I have said more than once in this book, you must get rid of all inhibitors to your goal achievement while remaining realistic. Above all, you can never give up hope of achieving your personal dreams for happiness. Being a parent in your thirties, or at any age, is not easy but, thanks to modern medicine, it is a healthy endeavor for mother and child in most cases. I thank God every day for my two little miracles. A cousin of mine had a healthy pregnancy in her early forties with medical assistance and has an adorable little girl as living proof. Although she used non-traditional conception, the result was a true miracle of life using modern medicine and a lot of faith. All children deserve happy homes with a parent or parents who want them and will love them unconditionally.

There are professionals out there who can help you reach your personal life goals once you figure out what direction you are going in and what you are trying to achieve in your life. Every major decision that I have made in my adult life has been made after a lot of careful thought and planning, as I outlined previously in Chapter Four. Society can impact our goal attainment in various ways. The "Mommy Wars" are a perfect example of societal and feminist norms interfering with women's personal choices. Some of the strongest feminists I have ever met have left the career track to be at-home parents. One of these women is the person I see every time that I look in the mirror. The choice for me was circumstantial and very personal. I thought to myself, *Scott just received a promotion at his job. My husband, God, and modern medicine have just given me the privilege of motherhood. Am I going to spend my child's early years teaching other children to read, write, and speak? Or am I going to be an at-home full-time mother for my own child?*

I asked myself these types of questions over and over again in the days immediately after the birth of my first daughter, Sedona. It was one of the most emotionally charged , soul-searching decisions that I have ever had to make for myself, my students, and my family. My decision would create a transition for my one hundred and two students who, before Sedona, were like my own children. The conclusion that I reached was to have another teacher finish the school year in my place.

My students were more understanding than I thought they would be, since they were eighth graders. Sometimes children in this age group can be quick to judge and ready to cut others down to size if they feel rejected. I dropped in to the classroom every other week to check on how the school year was progressing. It was important for me to have my daughter meet the other children that I cared so deeply for. I had known my students longer than she had been outside of the womb. The children adored Sedona and she was also very fond of them. She never cried when my former students or co-workers held her. Like her Mommy, she too got great enjoyment out of meeting people and making new friends.

Sedona attended Promotion Day with me. The students were ready for high school. Many of my students posed with me for photos, allowing me to hold a baby brother or sister. It was such a joy to see the confident expressions on their faces. They were young adults ready to advance to the next level, educationally. I hope they never forget what wonderful writers, speakers, and readers that I knew them to be. There is nothing better for a teacher than when a former student visits you at the school or within the community to tell you what's new in their worlds. Those meetings are usually happy ones and are one of the rewards of teaching. It is a big ego boost to hear former students tell you how they are using what you taught them to do well, in high school or life.

One of my students told me that she was going into social work because she loved my stories about being a case manager. She wanted to help people to live better for a living. Every one of my students inspired me. My job was simply to expand their young minds and promote their self-esteem while improving their understanding of how to improve their use of the English language. If I inspired any of them in even the slightest way, then I did my job. I hope to return to the classroom in the future.

*Chapter Seventeen*

No female part is exactly alike. Male parts are no more important than female ones.

There is currently a bit of a social battle going on between stay-at-home mothers and working mothers. Nobody really bothers at-home fathers because it is wonderful that his spouse is making enough money to support the family. That spouse is usually a woman, which pleases feminists like myself. I do not think it is necessary to create conflict between two different situations or choices in motherhood. Some women cannot stay at home for financial reasons. Some mothers are at home because of the same financial bind, only under different circumstances. It is my belief that a true feminist supports every woman's choices in regard to personal parenting preferences or work requirements in relation to motherhood. Whether that work is paid or unpaid, each one is a working mother, so I do not see the need for friction between the at-home moms or moms that work out of the home and seek child care.

The one thing that I cannot tolerate from other parents is the failure to monitor their child's behavior at public parks or community events. My friends and I call this OPK, or "Other People's Kids," syndrome in order to prevent open criticism of any emotionally numb, oblivious, or irresponsible caregiver. I shouldn't have to discipline someone else's child at the playground when the parent is ignoring his or her offspring. The following is a note to *laissez-faire* parents: The world is not your babysitter or nanny. You are fully responsible for your child's socially-inappropriate, obnoxious behavior toward other children during social interaction.

My mother, whom I consider a feminist, stayed at home with my brother and me until we were in kindergarten for half of the day. I do not believe that her six years of part-time employment and full-time motherhood was in vain or did harm to the women's movement. Staying at home to parent children is a huge endeavor requiring financial resources, personal and financial sacrifices, and a loss of pension benefits as a result of stepping down from the career ladder. It is the parenting gains that I am in it for. I know how fortunate I am to have a situation where I am not the sole income earner. Single mothers are some of the strongest women I know.

Stay-at-home mothers do not live in a vacuum. As children of the late 70s and 80s, most of us had a mother at home full-time until we went to grade school all day. It is not a slap in the face of feminism or the women's movement, as it appalls me to hear women say. One of my political colleagues wrote an editorial calling stay-at-home mothers "parasites" who feed off their significant others. I confronted her by saying, "Is that what you think of me, too?" She hugged me and said, "No, I don't." I said to her, "Unless you are a mother yourself, you shouldn't be so quick to judge. Didn't your mother stay at home with you? You turned out to be a real success story, just as much of a success as if your mother had worked full-time out of the home."

Many stay-at-home moms have college degrees and plan to use them as soon as their children are in grade school. Some women have quit working because they could not afford daycare for their children. Some mothers went to college on state assistance because they did not have a partner or because a deadbeat dad was involved. These women do well because many colleges assist with childcare costs by offering free or discounted childcare through the college.

All of these women are feminists in every sense of the word, because they are strong maternal role models who are taking full responsibility for the parenting of their children, making financial and social sacrifices, if necessary, to do so.

Unless a woman has children, she really has no right to judge another woman's choice to stay at home or to rush back to work with childcare assistance. Every woman is different. Every woman has a unique work or financial situation. All women deserve credit for raising happy, healthy children regardless of the number of hours in a day they physically spend with their infants or toddlers. I believe that parenting time, no matter what the actual time spent, should be focused on spending quality time with your children and making that shared time meaningful for parent and child through various age appropriate activities.

My choice does not suit all women, but I am happy that I chose to be an at-home mother. We should all be happy that we live in a country where women have so many choices. The only problem with the choice to be a stay-at-home mother is that for too many women doing so is not even an option. Employers tell many women that if they don't quickly come back to work after having a child they'll be fired, knocked down the pay scale a few steps, be replaced, or get reassigned. We should all work to even the playing field for mothers who would like to be at home but cannot do so for financial reasons. Our country does not give working mothers the support they need to be productive and the societal marginalization of mothers in the "Mommy Wars" must come to an end.

The women's movement must include all women, or we women will not gain the political momentum needed to finally pass the ERA and finally get the equal pay and career opportunities that men currently have. The most recent wage study by the U.S. Department of Labor concludes that a woman still makes only 78.3 cents of each dollar that a man makes (according to www.bls.gov). That is ridiculous. Our fight cannot be focused only on marital status, sexual orientation, motherhood or socioeconomic status.

To have all of our most important issues addressed, our fight has to be for all women to receive equal treatment among men and the respect that all women deserve throughout our society and the world. All women must come to the table in support of women's rights if we are to get the men in positions of power to listen to us in regard to finally adopting the ERA in all fifty states. How else will we ever have equal footing in our society?

My mother taught me that I can never have too many friends and not to be judgmental with my friends or my relationships would be paper thin and I would not get needed support in a pinch. I have found this piece of advice to be very valuable in all aspects of my life. Luckily, I do not place certain status, financial, or aesthetic requirements on my friendships. I could never be that shallow. My male and female friends are varied and wonderful. I like them for who they are and vice-versa.

Let me say that trust is a major element of any of my adult relationships. If someone breaks my trust once, he or she most likely will not get a second chance unless he or she is below the age of eighteen or a family member. There isn't enough time on this planet to concern myself with men or women who betray me. I am a Christian, therefore I forgive. I am intelligent, therefore I do not forget. My father taught me the following when I was a teenager: "If somebody crosses you once, he or she will most likely do it again. Don't let them do it again or you will wind up the fool, not the person who crossed you." He also had a self-defense rule that he explained to me and my brother as soon as he thought we could understand it. The self-defense rule was: "Don't ever start a fight, however if someone causes you intentional physical harm, you have my blessing to fight back the best that you can in self-defense." That was my Dad, the fighting Irishman who was not going to have his children bullied at school or anywhere else. My father also told me that I could do anything a boy or man could do, even better. His early influence pushed me to join the U.S. Army as he had after high school graduation.

Dad never expected me to join the Army. Nor was he pleased when he found out that I had signed up halfway through my junior year of high school. It was unusual for a young woman with excellent grades at my Catholic high school to enlist in the military. I was a college-bound student from a middle class family. None of that mattered. Our country was at war in the Middle East and I felt an irrepressible call to duty. Truth be told, I was a tougher and a better shot than many of my male counterparts. Becoming an Army Sharpshooter was no easy transition for a fashion-obsessed young woman from rural coastal Rhode Island. The Army was my introduction to many different regional dialects, ethnicities, and cultures that were all beautiful in their own way. We came from all walks of life.

One of my most interesting tech school classmates was worth millions, literally. Imagine an Army enlistee like Adelaide. Her father was an international real estate broker worth many millions of dollars. He would send her the newest, prettiest Rolexes for her birthdays when we were stationed in Germany. Her birthday celebration during training was an expensive, catered event courtesy of her family. There was a sheet cake of the American flag that was literally enough to feed everyone in our logistics company at Fort Lee. It was two picnic tables long with hundreds of tiny U.S. flags sticking out of the icing. The drill sergeants called her "Warbucks" which was a spoof and very close to the spelling of her actual surname. It was like being in the military with a real little orphan Annie. Whatever "Addie" wanted, Addie got.

She told me that her life of privilege got her in trouble with substance abuse and the law. Her schooling at a private boarding school in Massachusetts had been ample, yet emotionally cold. The one thing that boarding school never provided, she said, was family. Therefore, she had joined the Army to clean herself up and build her own "family." She was a great Army friend. When she was chosen for the cease fire in Saudi Arabia, Addie's Dad sent a stretch limo to take her and a bunch of our company members to eat dinner with a real Saudi prince, a real estate friend of her father's, at his palace. When those who do not know any better say that the military is nothing but a bunch of poor, underachieving, non-intellectual young men and women I just shake my head and set the record straight. It is truly unbearable to hear soldiers callously categorized in a negative way, making them even more foreign to the average American citizen. The media and too many years of extreme conservative propaganda and censorship has reduced the American image of war in Iraq and of our nation's soldiers to a few photos of smiling unharmed soldiers at photo-ops during the holidays, or with state and foreign dignitaries. These photo-ops burn me because some have been exposed as having been rehearsed and do not portray the true general situation of the majority of wartime troops.

Our people need to see the unrehearsed harsh actual war zone and war wounded footage. The result may be that the rush to war will not be so hastily done in the future. Many of us like to take the emotion out of discussions concerning war and our troops to minimize a collective guilty conscience for the human destruction on both sides. We need more reporters like those in the Vietnam era, like ousted CBS anchor Dan Rather who went to the frontlines to show America what was really happening on our battlefields in the Middle East, Afghanistan, and elsewhere in the world. It is time to re-sensitize our citizens about the cold reality of our foreign relations disaster under Bush and the human costs of Middle Eastern oil dependency.

If Americans banded together as they did in Nixon's time, we wouldn't worry about Presidential approval ratings because Bush would have lost his job due to sheer incompetence across the board. I am still waiting for G.W. to make one significant positive contribution of any kind to our nation's future. Even Nixon signed the Endangered Species Act of 1973, which was important in providing funding to protect our nation's vulnerable creatures great and small. Our former President has to stop expecting us and the rest of the world to compensate for his apparent lack of humanity in regard to our wars and our own domestic crises, as well as international regions of social and political unrest. Our past President has a definite lack of foreign relations skills that lost us allies and respect around the globe. While George W. Bush was in the White House, he refused to face our nation's educational and economic inadequacies, which are now both at crisis level.

Bush was not alone in his "political detachment disorder." Our country is largely being run by incredibly disconnected men and women, with mostly men having the most powerful positions. Too many politicians no longer mingle with their constituents and are continually preoccupied with the next fundraiser or house party. I am not saying that the fundraising is not important, because it is. That said, equal time has to be allocated to those who cannot donate to the campaign fund, those who most likely depend on the government the most to be organized and fully functioning.

The reasons elected officials sometimes give for being out of touch with the community are varied. Some officials reek of self-importance. Some appear uncomfortable and act as though they are somehow being inconvenienced by "troubled" citizens in their care. Most do not make time for a planned visit from a constituent without so much as an explanation, nor do many reschedule meetings or even the public appearances. Some government meetings are scheduled during the day midweek to eliminate any public discussion of a civic matter that directly affects the constituency. This not uncommon treatment makes the public distrusting and creates feelings of disappointment toward their local and federal political figures. Too many of our citizens have been silenced for too long.

When I ran for office in the fall of 2005 for the November 2006 election cycle, I saw a lot of apathetic reactions to citizens from public officials who I thought could get along with and listen to just about anyone. Some seemed to want to cherry-pick the topic of conversation a few seconds after an uncomfortable topic of discussion was brought up. Too many Americans are indirectly silenced by political band-aids like "No Child Left Behind." When I taught in the public schools, we teachers called it "Every Child Left Behind." It offered just enough funding to quiet the public education community, slightly, for the short term. No direct funding went to further qualify teachers in their chosen subject areas or grade levels, leaving them on their own to meet new requirements. If they did not meet new and improved criteria after a certain prescribed length of time, they lost their positions. I worked with a math teacher with a Master's Degree from an African university who was told under No Child Left Behind that he did not have the formal U.S. education requirements to remain a math teacher. Mind you, he had been a professor in Nigeria before moving to our country.

No additional federal funding went into improving science and technology programs to help make our American children global contenders. Our country is number twelve out of the eighteen wealthiest nations worldwide in educating children. Grade school learners in the United States have a quality of education that lags behind the learners in, from order of best to worst: Belgium, Canada, Poland, Finland, Sweden, Netherlands, Ireland, Denmark, the Czech Republic, Germany, and Norway according to the most recent Unicef world report card on children's well being (www.unicef.org) and detailed extensively at: http://www.unicef-icdc.org/publications/pdf/rc7_eng.pdf . I would say that our nation's educational system is in need of a lot of much more attention, funding, and restructuring to be where it needs to be, at the top of the world's wealthiest nations for education. If we put the $15 billion dollars per month that has been going to sustain the Iraqi occupation into improving our children's quality of education we would have the best education system in the world, period. There is no question that to protect the future of our country we must properly advance education for all of our citizens.

As a mother, military veteran, former social worker, and former teacher, I saw a major disconnect between our citizens and their political leaders. I began to consider running for office. This political disconnectedness became my call to action. I threw my hat in for the Arizona State House of Representatives for the 2006 election cycle with my two daughters ages two-and-a-half and one year-old in my care. Some thought I was insane to run for state office with two small children at home, but I felt that I had no choice.

I became heavily involved in the Democratic Party soon after becoming an at-home parent when John Kerry was running for President. I decided to join the Greater Eastern Maricopa Democrats, or "GemDems," to help canvass local neighborhoods. I was in my second trimester of my second pregnancy. Canvassing was an effective way to get doctor-approved exercise to stay healthy. Canvassing also gave me the opportunity to remain politically-active and to encourage voter participation within my community.

I find canvassing a rewarding activity because I get a chance to connect with my neighbors and find out their perspectives on American politics whether they share my political views or not. Many of my neighbors including blue- and white-collar workers had unmanageable health insurance costs, had to apply for state assistance due to inability to pay, or had no health coverage at all. Grown men and women would break down in tears over their frustration with our nation's current broken healthcare system. Some were terminally ill because they had gotten necessary medical attention too late.

Children suffered from treatable health conditions but were left without treatment because of a parent or guardian's financial situation. Many parents lacked knowledge regarding SHIPP (the State Children's Health Insurance Program) or other healthcare programs for our nation's little ones lacking coverage whose parents or guardians cannot afford private insurance and do not qualify for state assistance because the family brings in annual income above the poverty line. I met a lot of folks who lacked transportation to get to the organizations that could help them medically. It seems that poverty remains the worst pre-existing condition in the United States when it comes to our citizens' overall health.

Everyone in 2004 was tired of the Iraq war, yet was not yet angry enough about having been lied to by President Bush and his "weapons of mass destruction" hoax. *Where was the outrage?* It was apparent that families in Mesa were more concerned with their daily survival than with Iraq. The level of hopelessness and mistrust of government was a consistent conversation piece at households of any political affiliation. Even many Republicans, Libertarians, and unaffiliated Independents were unhappy with the Patriot Act language, as it interfered with their Constitutional right to privacy. How can any President arbitrarily tweak our U.S. Constitution to intercept our private conversations via any form of communication without a warrant?

Presidential and vice-presidential candidates John Kerry and John Edwards had a lot of voter apathy in Arizona to remedy. Although a progressive state, Arizona has a Republican majority in its state legislature and in Congress. Many Mesa Republicans that I came in contact with felt somewhat put off by Bush, but thought Kerry did not address terrorism and the terrorist acts of September eleventh as much as they thought he should. Bush was still their "patron" saint because our nation still had post-9/11 stress with multicolored terror level alerts on the television daily. I am happy that those alerts virtually disappeared after Bush's re-election. It is 2008, and I wonder why Bush isn't bombarding us with the terror alerts again.

The obstacles to voting were many. Some men and women were told that they would not be allowed to vote during the workday or would risk repercussions from their employers. I told them that that employer behavior was illegal, but they told me that they could not afford to fight their employer's refusal to let them vote. Many had no idea how to request, or properly fill out, a mail-in ballot. Some had not heard of early voting. We gave helpful hints about getting to the polls, poll hours, and due dates for their mail-in ballots. The worst product of voter apathy was the high number of men and women who were not registered to vote. They had no idea how to register, so we would give the forms out like hotcakes, even to Republicans and Independents, because we live in a democracy and every vote must count.

As the months went by, the "Swift Boat Veterans" quagmire came up. Kerry did not quickly respond in his own defense and the public was questioning his toughness under political fire, even make-believe fire as it was. We GemDems did not waver in our support for Kerry and Edwards. There was a collective feeling of satisfaction stemming from our raising of voter awareness at every doorstep. I enjoyed being a good will ambassador for the upcoming election.

It felt as though 2004 would be the year that we Democrats would have a highly-intelligent, innovative, thoughtful President in John Kerry, with the added bonus of the smart, stylish, super-charged champion of the blue-collar workers, John Edwards for Vice President. They both had strong family values, at that time anyway on Edward's part, and tight-knit families. We would not have another somber Al Gore-type seemingly stolen presidential election. When Al Gore stopped fighting, it was a sobering call to action for every Democrat. We could not allow these voter tally errors and voter disenfranchisement episodes to happen again. I felt that, if the election was close, Kerry would beat George Bush.

Finally, Election Day came and the vote numbers were so close that there were hand counts in progress in states where Diebold voting machine glitches had been alleged, particularly in Ohio and, surprise, Florida, home of Bush brother Jeb. Voter fraud charges were being levied from sea to shining sea. Minority groups in Florida and elsewhere were livid after claiming that they were turned away at the polls because poll workers lied about the polls being closed. Similar stories were told elsewhere. Voter fraud was supposed to happen only in corrupt third world countries, under communism or fascism. *Was this the land of the free and the home of the brave, or had we become the land of the fooled and cowardly?*

Where was the fight for our right to have our votes counted to preserve our democracy? Weren't Americans afraid to lose their civil liberties and the American dream as a consequence of having lost their voices in the 2004 election? How could so many Americans be de-sensitized to their own well-being as it relates to government corruption? Why were soldiers putting their lives on the line for a President who lied to Congress to restart his dad's war with Saddam Hussein? Why couldn't President Bush use diplomatic efforts to improve our standing around the world, particularly in oil-producing countries?

These questions have a wide range of answers as diverse as the American people. Nixon was impeached for committing the same types of attacks on democracy and the citizens of the United States forced him to step down. Today's America simply complains without taking decisive action. We just look at the latest poll numbers related to approval ratings. Bush's have been lower than President Nixon's worst approval rating. What has weakened American pride so much that we will turn a blind eye to the corrupt actions of some of our elected officials?

I simply will not rest until Americans once again unite to better our democracy from the top on down. Americans must fight against oppressive federal and state legislation. We must protect our American freedoms and the pursuit of happiness by taking elected officials to task regarding the issues that are near and dear to our hearts. We must be heard on legislation that affects how we live. Quality of life got Americans to the polls decades ago due to concern for themselves and their family members. Voting was seen more as a duty required of every American citizen. Who or what is to blame for most Americans sitting democracy out?

Voters cannot afford to be bench warmers as we are seeing in the endless Iraq and Afganistan conflicts and an unprecedented mortgage crisis. Are we all awake, yet? Some media sources are filtering the truth so much that it is unrecognizable. Others do a good job of presenting the not-so-pleasant realities of American life. An alternate reality is played out on television, on the radio, and in many of the newspapers that we read. The truth needs to gain more popularity or we are all going to suffer for it. Sensationalism regarding politician's sex lives, psychopathic creeps, and non-news stories are on the front page or given the most air time. A little dirty laundry goes a long way. Issues that are affecting us the most are getting obscure back of the front page mini-columns and tiny sound bites. We must demand more useful and accurate information from our major news sources.

*Chapter Eighteen*

My engine is revved up.
I'm ready to run.

One of the main reasons that I decided to run for office was to help restore trust between voters and their elected officials. I had no ulterior motives for wanting to be a state representative. I had clear reasons to run that concerned the quality of life for the people living in my legislative district and the entire state. There was no Democratic Party-affiliated representation at the state level in my district and there had not been for about a decade. Democrats were greatly outnumbered in most departments of Mesa city government. Mesa government needed more of a political balance. The governor faced re-election in a race that she was 99.9% sure of winning because of her successes with vetoing legislation that would have greatly diminished the standard of living in Arizona and hurt Arizona families. The main problem was a lack of Democratic support in the Republican majority state legislature. Any progressive legislation was being blocked, with some bills never seeing the light of day in committee.

Arizona's schools kept competing for last place nationally against Utah for the lowest per-student spending, at around $3,000.00 per student when I taught. I did the breakdown of the funding over the school year and it was dismal. Only 2 cents per day went to school nutrition. What kind of food does two cents get a child to eat for lunch? Each year teachers would spend hundreds of dollars to stock pens, pencils, and lined paper to supplement the school's supply room. We teachers had pencils, pens, and paper rationed to us. Either we bought the supplies ourselves out of our paychecks, or the students didn't get them. Education bills were too often watered down, which effected every student and teacher in Arizona's broken public school system.

Arizona's healthcare system was a mess. People were waiting upwards of twelve hours for equipment in the waiting rooms because of archaic malpractice laws that scared physicians out of the state's emergency rooms. Seniors and small children suffered the most from emergency room overcrowding. Arizona has one of the highest rates of uninsured men, women, and children in the country, which has financially strained the state's general fund and has saturated the state's assistance rolls.

Small business owners were hurting. I had spoken to many small business owners as a precinct committeeperson before I ran. The business owners complained that Mesa did not have a business-friendly climate, with overregulation on advertising and fears that, without tax breaks or other incentives for healthcare benefits, many of them would have to lay off employees or go out of business. Many business owners said that without tax relief, they could not last much longer. The Mom-and-Pops were in real trouble. I have always been a staunch supporter of local business and it bothered me to see the entrepreneurial spirit hampered by a lack of state support and overregulation by the city and state which mostly favored only large companies. The playing field for business had to be leveled. Everyone had to follow the same business rules whether they liked it or not. Small businesses deserve as much a chance as the largest franchise does.

I also think businesses that follow state and federal immigration laws, and offer competitive wages with healthcare benefits should be rewarded for being so conscientious. Union-affiliated businesses already do these things, but too many others do not. Immigration was another reason for my running. My great-grandparents had to apply for citizenship, learn English, and follow the laws of the land. Some immigrants are skipping the signing-up-for-citizenship part of becoming a citizen. Having a green card or visa should be a source of pride. The immigrant visa was something my great-grandparents held in high regard because it meant that they would someday be American citizens. They just had to work hard, not break the law, and learn the English language.

Many immigrants still follow those basic rules by immediately signing up for citizenship. Some immigrants aren't signing up for citizenship and some of those folks are dangerous criminals who are without any identification. Border crime was so bad in Arizona that the governor had to send the Army National Guard in to get a handle on border violence. When the Arizona guard was exhausted, the governor at the time, Janet Napolitano who is now President Barack Obama's Secretary of Homeland Security, had to rally then President George W. Bush to get more National Guard troops out on the border to protect our citizens, their livestock, and their homes. Another good reason to decrease the number of illegal immigrant crossings is that many die due to crossing the border through the hot desert. Yet another excellent reason for immigration reform is that when governments put illegal immigrant parents in jail, they displace and destroy the lives of their children. Children do not get to choose their parents. We all must remember that when helping to reform our immigration laws. The United States does not need high walls along borders, only effective security systems and well-trained personnel who can manage the flow of attempted illegal crossings. All immigrants must possess a work visa or should be deported.

My great-grandparents followed the rules, learned enough English to provide for their families, and eventually gained citizenship. I believe that all immigrants should get their green cards and work to become citizens as has been done successfully since

1924. Immigrants should have to work for citizenship or go elsewhere to a country where failing to register is legally acceptable. As an 8th grade English teacher in Phoenix, Arizona, I saw too often how an unregistered immigrant parent could splinter a family to dysfunction overnight. I remember the tears of my students whose parents were being deported for lack of citizenship documentation.

No children should be placed in such a life-altering situation, left to other relatives or the foster care system to remain in the country they were born in. Keeping families who migrate to the U.S. together is important, however there must be an organized immigration system to deal with law-abiding immigrants who simply want a better life for their families. My hope is that new state and federal immigration laws will take into account families that are currently contributing to our economy and obey the law. I believe that violent criminals from foreign countries should be deported and serve their time in their country of origin, with all of our related costs paid for by that country of origin. This would help to eliminate costs of housing illegal immigrant convicts in our jails and prisons. Legal immigrants work too hard to have illegal immigrants receive cuts in the long immigration line due to failure to follow the rules. Our immigration system has to grow up to fit today's immigration issues. Every person living in our country must have identification in order to help prevent crime and identify "nameless" anonymous crime victims of all ages across our country.   Realistically, our country cannot afford to finance every illegal immigrant who slips beneath the radar. It is time for honesty among our nation's immigrants. We need an honest effort by all immigrants to become naturalized citizens and to pay their state and federal taxes as all Americans do.

Tax-paying Americans cannot continue to provide for every refugee hiding within our borders who is unwilling to work toward citizenship. These unwilling refugees should either sign up or please move on. Signing up for U.S. citizenship is the correct thing for an immigrant to do. U.S. citizenship is worth waiting for and working toward. The U.S. is not able to finance every indigent foreigner, nor can our private and government-run agencies afford the billions in lost funds in the process of being humane to the undocumented. We must be humane, yet realistic, about how far our country should extend itself until better immigration guidelines are developed. Bring us your tired, your poor, and tempest tossed. In addition, make sure that they have the integrity to make themselves known as immigrants, to carry an immigration photo ID, work documentation, and a willingness to enter into our nation's immigration system to track their progress up the citizenship ladder. This may all seem like common sense, yet I have seen no bi-partisan agreement on any new immigrant visa or citizenship course of action passed by our Congress. What I have seen is a lot of intense bickering back and forth while some illegal immigrants wrinkle their noses and hope to avoid detection.

Immigrants wait in the shadows unsure of their future as border security threatens the safety and financial well-being of a nation. It is ineffective teamwork at its worst that keeps immigration issues on the backburner. Some business owners are choosing the cheap, unregulated labor as a result of greed, instead of an ethical on-the-books legal citizenship route for their employees. In the meantime, illegal immigrants drive down the wages of American citizens in similar jobs and face on-the-job mistreatment. Immigrants in the shadows will work in much worse conditions for much less pay than your average American, even on wages that most Americans could not make a living with. As the great-granddaughter of Irish and Italian immigrants, I can tell you that they learned English, worked very hard at the least glamorous jobs, and managed to survive the legal immigration process unscathed. Every immigrant should still have to go through a similar process, except with more modern ID and data collection systems in place.

The support that I had for my state legislative race was unexpected and phenomenal. My endorsements were numerous and dwarfed those of my opponents. They didn't feel that they had to work that hard, so I worked even harder. I picked up major state and national endorsements. I received endorsements from the Arizona AFL-CIO, the Arizona Federation of State, County, and Municipal Employees (AFSCME), the National Association of Social Workers, the Arizona Correctional Peace Officers' Association, the Arizona Women's Political Caucus, the Arizona League of Conservation Voters, Planned Parenthood of Arizona, the Arizona Human Rights Fund, the pre-scandal Arizona Association of Community Organizations for Reform Now (ACORN), and the not-so-well-known, but no less important, Modified Motorcycle Association (MMA) of Arizona. It was an honor to be chosen to represent these wonderful organizations.

I had weathered my opponents' underhanded comments and one overly aggressive handshake from my younger opponent before a debate. I had forgotten to shake his hand at our city-sponsored debate. During our mandatory Clean Elections debate, the younger opponent had a mother who reacted to my remarks by spasmodically leaping up and down from her seat like a jack-in-the-box. At every political challenge I posed to her son, she would look like a wildcat ready to pounce. After debates, this mother would make passive-aggressive remarks, such as "It's all going to come out in the wash" within earshot of me and then would glare at me as I walked past. The apple didn't fall far from the tree.

My other opponent was a handsome smooth-talking narcissistic man who would agree with me in debate in an attempt to appear moderate when he definitely wasn't, continually tried to look at my hand-written notes, and would attempt to steal my thunder, unsuccessfully, by making distracting off-topic remarks about something unrelated to the moderator's questions. My two opponents would say or do anything in a sexist attempt to show a contrived male superiority over me and to try to distort my strong mainstream message. By election time, I was a lot better received by the district's citizens, as well as local, state, and federal organizations, than they ever imagined I would be. As I had promised my supporters, my opponents would face a tough battle up to, and on Election Day.

After nearly winning a tight race, I, along with my husband, had some serious thinking to do. I decided that I would rather not spend the next several years, and many thousands of dollars to run again in Arizona. I would not easily leave Mesa. My husband became aware of a new opportunity for him on the East Coast. We were both ready for new challenges.

I missed the East Coast, particularly the northeastern United States, where most of my extended family lived. Mesa was experiencing a huge financial dilemma. City libraries were opened for fewer hours. City-sponsored community events such as holiday lights and parades would no longer be affordable. There were fewer courses offered for the children through parks and recreation, which I viewed as a revenue-builder and, yet, were being cancelled at an alarming rate. Scott and I had had enough of lack of community-building and a grim local municipal financial forecast. The city's mayor and the all-conservative, predominately-male city council with only one female member, were paralyzed under recession. It was becoming unbearable to watch. Scott and I decided to look elsewhere in pursuit of our American dream.

*Chapter Nineteen*

There has to be something in my tool kit that will prevent clogs in my dream machine.

It was very difficult to leave some of the best friends, political supporters, and family members that one could ever hope and pray for, that I was blessed to have. That said, it was still time to move on for the life that we always wanted for our children, like the time we had spent as children in four seasons and quiet communities like Scott's childhood in Sioux Falls, South Dakota, and mine in Charlestown, Rhode Island. Scott took a transfer to Maryland. We decided to buy a house in Montgomery County, Maryland, a place with a lot of diversity, where citizens have true representation evident through many civic groups and highly-accessible elected officials. Most county funding goes into education, first responders, and affordable housing, which are all important during a national economic downturn now commonly referred to as "The Great Recession." The schools have consistently been in the top ten of all states for decades for educational excellence. As a politico, I enjoy being close to Washington, DC and its nation-sustaining heartbeat. As a nineteen-year-old soldier, I was flown Medevac from Germany to Walter Reed Army Medical Center for foot surgery. I remember the clean, cheerful halls of Walter Reed with the pomp and circumstance of the officers with their intricate uniforms and shiny brass.

The colonel who operated on my foot was a top-notch podiatrist who treated me as though I were one of his family members, not merely an injured enlisted subordinate.

The doctor gave me medical administrative duties to complete before and after surgery because in his words, "a mind is a terrible thing to waste." As a reward for my hard work organizing his files, I received a Christmas card from my thoughtful Jewish podiatrist. It was a touching gesture. It was a beautiful card made all the more beautiful by his extending a religious greeting toward me that was unrelated to his own religious views. When I opened the card I found passes to the officer's lap pool "to strengthen [my] foot and get some physical conditioning before heading back to Germany." He had also included a brand new crisp one hundred dollar bill as payment for helping him to organize his new office. The gratitude that I felt toward this Army colonel was overwhelming. Dr. Yanklovitch cared about soldier's limbs *and* hearts. My experience as a young surgery patient was a challenging, yet bright, interlude to the day-to-day grind of being an active duty soldier in Bitburg, Germany, where I was stationed. I had been disappointed about my broken foot, but it got me to Washington, DC, and thanks to the United States Army and the USO I got to experience a lot of the beauty and culture of the nation's capitol and had fallen in love with it.

The DC area and I feel like old friends. It is great to be back. Many ask me, "Are you going to run for office again?" Being in political office is one of my dreams, so you can bet that I will most likely run again. Until then, I am going to help my community members and my country in any way that I can. I will also remain involved in organizations that help men, women, and children abroad. It is something that I feel it is my responsibility to do. As the daughter of a woman who held elected office, I would like her to be able to pass the torch of public service on to me. It would be my pleasure and privilege to do so.

## Chapter Twenty:

## Effectively Maintaining Your Superstructure by Using Your Personal Tool Kit for Life.

Now that you have created your Personal Tool Kit for Life, you should be feeling a lot better prepared for the repairs you must make along life's path. You know what steps to take to reach your chosen destination, not the path chosen by friends, family, or acquaintances, but a path of your very own. You now own your life and possess the skills to properly manage whatever crises come your way.

You have carefully developed your plan for a stronger self. This is a huge accomplishment. The reward for working so diligently toward self-improvement should be satisfaction and goal achievement. Remember that your life repairs will not bring you instant gratification. Life's successes do not happen overnight.

You have the tools in your personal tool kit to overcome any obstacle in the way of reaching the life goals that mean the most to your success in life and your personal happiness. These tools are now a part of you and will stay with you as long as you use them often and effectively to achieve your goals, whatever they may be. I doubt you will ever exclaim, "I can't do this!" again, or if you even think about it revisit the tools you have accumulated in your personal tool kit, strategize about how you will absolutely complete the task at hand, and construct a better life than you thought could be possible.

Once we learn from where we have been, it is much easier to continue moving ahead, excited for what tomorrow brings, instead of being paralyzed by fear and self-doubt. Learn from the past, but do not remain immobile within it. Keep moving forward.

You now have the tools. Use them. You have worked hard to obtain them. Repair yourself as needed and if you ever get those lonely, helpless, distraught feelings again…you know, that loose screw…open that emergency self-esteem kit. Start feeling the love and admiration for yourself. I wish you only the best as you begin, or continue, on the path to realizing your dreams. I sincerely hope and pray that they all come true. Never give up. Your happiness is way too important. Remember to carry your crisis list with you. Don't forget to bring along your emergency self-esteem and personal tool kits. You will need them. Everyone does.

# About the Author

The author earned a Bachelor of Science degree in Human Development and Family Studies at the University of Rhode Island. Lara is a military veteran, former social work case manager, 8th grade Language Arts teacher, and 2006 candidate for Arizona State Representative. She currently serves on several boards, her civic association, PTA, as well as numerous memberships in advocacy groups locally, nationally, and globally. Lara is thirty-seven years old and is married to her soul mate Scott. She and her husband have three children. The author and her family reside in Maryland.